TALHA WAQAS

Excel Step by Step

*From Dummies To Professional, The Most Updated and
Complete 2023 Guide to Charm Your Boss, Save Time
and Make Your Life Easy.*

First edition

ISBN: 9798856358239

This book was professionally typeset on Reedsy.
Find out more at reedsy.com

Contents

Introduction to Excel 2023   1

  Why Use Excel 2023 ?   1

  1.1. What is Excel 2023?   3

  1.2. Installing Excel 2023   3

  1.3. Understanding the Excel Interface   4

  1.4. Basic Excel Terminology   5

  1.5. Setting Up Your First Spreadsheet   5

  Interactive Exercises   7

Chapter 2: Navigating the Excel Interface   8

  2.1. Understanding the Ribbon   8

  2.2. Working with the Quick Access Toolbar   9

  2.3. Managing Views   9

  2.4. Customizing the Excel Environment   10

  2.5. Using Help Features   11

  Interactive Exercises   11

Chapter 3: Creating and Saving Workbooks   12

  3.1. Creating New Workbooks   12

  3.2. Saving and Opening Workbooks   13

  3.3. Using Templates   13

  3.4. AutoRecover and AutoSave   14

  3.5. Importing and Exporting Data   14

  Interactive Exercises   15

Chapter 4: Entering and Editing Data   16

  4.1. Inputting Data   16

4.2. Editing Cell Contents 17

4.3. Using AutoFill 17

4.4. Inserting and Deleting Cells, Rows,
and Columns 17

4.5. Copying and Moving Data 18

Interactive Exercises 19

Chapter 5: Working with Cells and Ranges 20

5.1. Selecting Cells and Ranges 20

5.2. Formatting Cells and Ranges 21

5.3. Using Styles and Themes 21

5.4. Cell Alignment and Text Wrapping 22

5.5. Merging and Splitting Cells 22

Interactive Exercises 23

Chapter 6: Managing Worksheets and Workbooks 24

6.1. Adding and Deleting Worksheets 24

6.2. Renaming and Moving Worksheets 25

6.3. Grouping and Ungrouping Worksheets 25

6.4. Hiding and Unhiding Worksheets 26

6.5. Linking Worksheets 26

Interactive Exercises 27

Case Study: Inventory Management for
a Small Retail Business 27

Chapter 7: Basic Formulas and Functions 28

7.1. Understanding Formulas 28

7.2. Using Basic Functions 29

7.3. Relative and Absolute Cell References 29

7.4. Using the Formula Auditing Tools 30

7.5. Troubleshooting Formulas 30

Interactive Exercises 31

Chapter 8: Advanced Formulas and Functions 32

8.1. Using Logical Functions 32

8.2. Using Lookup Functions 33

8.3. Using Date and Time Functions 33

8.4. Using Text Functions 34

8.5. Using Array Formulas 34

Interactive Exercises 35

Chapter 9: Working with Tables 36

9.1. Creating Tables 36

9.2. Formatting Tables 37

9.3. Sorting and Filtering Tables 38

9.4. Using Table References in Formulas 38

9.5. Converting Tables to Ranges 39

Interactive Exercises 39

Chapter 10: Data Validation and Conditional Formatting 40

10.1. Applying Data Validation 40

10.2. Creating Drop-Down Lists 41

10.3. Using Conditional Formatting 42

10.4. Managing Conditional Formatting Rules 42

10.5. Highlighting Cells with Conditional Formatting 43

Interactive Exercises 44

Chapter 11: Working with Charts 45

11.1 Creating Charts 45

11.2 Formatting Charts 46

11.3 Modifying Chart Elements 47

11.4 Creating Combination Charts 47

11.5 Creating Sparklines 48

Interactive Exercises 49

Chapter 12: Advanced Charting Techniques 50

12.1 Creating PivotCharts 50

12.2 Using the Quick Analysis Tool 51

12.3 Creating Histograms and Box and Whisker Charts ... 51

12.4 Creating Treemap and Sunburst Charts ... 52

12.5 Creating Waterfall and Funnel Charts ... 52

Interactive Exercises ... 53

Chapter 13: Working with PivotTables ... 54

13.1 Creating PivotTables: The Power of Summarized Data ... 54

13.2 Modifying PivotTables: Customizing Your Data View ... 55

13.3 Using Slicers and Timelines: Simplifying Data Filtering ... 56

13.4 Creating Calculated Fields and Items: Enhancing Your PivotTable ... 56

13.5 Creating PivotTables from Multiple Ranges: Connecting Data ... 57

Interactive Exercises ... 58

Chapter 14: Advanced PivotTable Techniques ... 59

14.1 Using Power Pivot: Extending Your Data Analysis ... 59

14.2 Creating Measures with DAX: Elevating Calculations ... 60

14.3 Using the Data Model: Unifying Data Sources ... 61

14.4 Creating Relationships Between Tables: Linking Your Data ... 61

14.5 Using Hierarchies in PivotTables: Structuring Your Data ... 62

Interactive Exercises ... 62

Chapter 15: Introduction to Power Query ... 63

15.1 Understanding Power Query: Bridging the Gap Between Data and Insight   63

15.2 Importing Data with Power Query: Simplifying Data Access   64

15.3 Cleaning and Transforming Data with Power Query: Unleashing Data's True Potential   65

15.4 Merging and Appending Queries: Streamlining Your Data Structure   65

15.5 Loading Queries to the Workbook: Completing the Data Preparation Journey   66

Interactive Exercises   66

Chapter 16: Advanced Power Query Techniques   67

16.1 Using the Query Editor   67

16.2 Creating Calculated Columns   68

16.3 Using Conditional Columns   68

16.4 Grouping and Aggregating Data   68

16.5 Using Parameters in Queries   69

Interactive Exercises   69

Chapter 17: Introduction to Power BI   70

17.1 Understanding Power BI: Redefining Data Analysis   70

17.2 Importing Data into Power BI: Laying the Groundwork   71

17.3 Creating Reports in Power BI: Translating Data into Insights   71

17.4 Publishing to the Power BI Service: Propagating Insights   72

17.5 Creating Dashboards in Power BI: Weaving a Data Story   72

Interactive Exercises   73
Chapter 18: Collaborating in Excel   74
    18.1 Sharing Workbooks: Elevating Teamwork   74
    18.2 Co-Authoring Workbooks: Har-
    nessing Collective Wisdom   75
    18.3 Protecting Workbooks and Work-
    sheets: Balancing Collaboration with
    Control   75
    18.4 Tracking Changes: Maintaining
    Accountability and Transparency   76
    18.5 Adding and Reviewing Comments:
    Streamlining Communication   76
    Interactive Exercises   77
Chapter 19: Automating Tasks with Macros   78
    19.1 Understanding Macros: The Back-
    bone of Excel Automation   78
    19.2 Recording Macros: Documenting
    Steps for Future Repetition   79
    19.3 Running and Editing Macros: Ef-
    fortless Execution and Modification   79
    19.4 Understanding VBA: The Driving
    Force of Excel Macros   80
    19.5 Creating Macros with VBA: Tailor-
    ing Automation to Your Needs   80
    Interactive Exercises   81
Chapter 20: Excel for Financial Analysis   82
    20.1 Using Financial Functions   82
    20.2 Building Financial Models   83
    20.3 Performing What-If Analysis   83
    20.4 Using the Analysis ToolPak   84
    20.5 Creating Amortization Schedules   84

Interactive Exercises   85
Chapter 21: Excel for Statistical Analysis   86
  21.1 Using Statistical Functions   86
  21.2 Analyzing Data with Descriptive Statistics   87
  21.3 Testing Hypotheses with Inferential Statistics   87
  21.4 Performing Regression Analysis   87
  21.5 Creating Probability Distributions   88
  Interactive Exercises   88
Chapter 22: Excel for Data Science   89
  22.1 Understanding the Data Science Process   89
  22.2 Cleaning and Preparing Data   90
  22.3 Exploratory Data Analysis in Excel   90
  22.4 Building Predictive Models in Excel   90
  22.5 Visualizing Data for Data Science   91
  Interactive Exercises   91
Chapter 23: Excel for Project Management   92
  23.1 Creating Gantt Charts   92
  23.2 Tracking Project Tasks   93
  23.3 Managing Resources   93
  23.4 Analyzing Project Costs   93
  23.5 Reporting Project Status   94
  Interactive Exercises   94
Chapter 24: Excel for Marketing   95
  24.1 Analyzing Market Trends   95
  24.2 Forecasting Sales   96
  24.3 Analyzing Customer Segments   96
  24.4 Tracking Campaign Performance   96
  24.5 Creating Dashboards for Marketing   97
  Interactive Exercises   98
Chapter 25: Excel for Human Resources   99
  25.1 Tracking Employee Data   99

25.2 Analyzing Employee Turnover 100

25.3 Creating Compensation Models 100

25.4 Analyzing Training and Development 100

25.5 Creating HR Dashboards 101

Interactive Exercises 102

Chapter 26: Excel for Supply Chain Management 103

26.1 Tracking Inventory 103

26.2 Analyzing Supplier Performance 104

26.3 Forecasting Demand 104

26.4 Optimizing Logistics 105

26.5 Creating Dashboards for Supply
Chain Management 105

Interactive Exercises 106

Chapter 27: Excel for Sales 107

27.1 Tracking Sales Data 107

27.2 Analyzing Sales Trends 108

27.3 Forecasting Sales 108

27.4 Analyzing Sales Performance 109

27.5 Creating Dashboards for Sales 109

Interactive Exercises 110

Chapter 28: Excel for Customer Service 111

28.1 Tracking Customer Service Data 111

28.2 Analyzing Customer Satisfaction 112

28.3 Analyzing Call Center Performance 112

28.4 Creating Service Level Agreements 113

28.5 Creating Dashboards for Customer Service 113

Interactive Exercises 114

Chapter 29: Excel for Operations 115

29.1 Tracking Operational Data 115

29.2 Analyzing Operational Efficiency 116

29.3 Creating Production Schedules 116

29.4 Analyzing Quality Control Data 117

29.5 Creating Dashboards for Operations 117

Interactive Exercises 118

Chapter 30: Excel for Accounting 119

30.1 Tracking Financial Data 119

30.2 Creating Financial Statements 120

30.3 Analyzing Financial Ratios 120

30.4 Performing Variance Analysis 121

30.5 Creating Dashboards for Accounting 121

Interactive Exercises 122

Chapter 31: Excel for Auditing 123

31.1 Tracking Audit Data 123

31.2 Performing Audit Tests 124

31.3 Analyzing Audit Results 124

31.4 Creating Audit Reports 124

31.5 Creating Dashboards for Auditing 125

Interactive Exercises 126

Chapter 32: Excel for Risk Management 127

32.1 Tracking Risk Data 127

32.2 Analyzing Risk Factors 128

32.3 Creating Risk Models 128

32.4 Performing Risk Assessments 129

32.5 Creating Dashboards for Risk Management 129

Interactive Exercises 130

Chapter 33: Excel for Quality Management 131

33.1 Tracking Quality Data 131

33.2 Analyzing Quality Metrics 132

33.3 Creating Quality Control Charts 132

33.4 Performing Root Cause Analysis 133

33.5 Creating Dashboards for Quality Management 133

Interactive Exercises 134

Chapter 34: Excel for Healthcare 135
34.1 Tracking Patient Data 135
34.2 Analyzing Health Outcomes 136
34.3 Creating Treatment Plans 136
34.4 Analyzing Healthcare Costs 137
34.5 Creating Dashboards for Healthcare 137
Interactive Exercises 138
Chapter 35: Excel for Education 139
35.1 Tracking Student Data 139
35.2 Analyzing Test Scores 140
35.3 Creating Lesson Plans 140
35.4 Analyzing School Performance 141
35.5 Creating Dashboards for Education 141
Interactive Exercises 142
Chapter 36: Excel for Real Estate 143
36.1 Tracking Property Data 143
36.2 Analyzing Market Trends 144
36.3 Creating Financial Models for Real Estate 144
36.4 Analyzing Property Investments 145
36.5 Creating Dashboards for Real Estate 145
Interactive Exercises 146
Chapter 37: Excel for Nonprofits 147
37.1 Tracking Donor Data 147
37.2 Analyzing Fundraising Campaigns 148
37.3 Creating Budgets for Nonprofits 148
37.4 Analyzing Program Outcomes 149
37.5 Creating Dashboards for Nonprofits 149
Interactive Exercises 150
Chapter 38: Excel for Personal Finance 151
38.1 Tracking Personal Finances 151
38.2 Creating Personal Budgets 152

38.3 Analyzing Investments   152

38.4 Planning for Retirement   153

38.5 Creating Dashboards for Personal Finance   153

Interactive Exercises   154

Chapter 39: Excel Tips and Tricks   155

39.1 Using Keyboard Shortcuts   155

39.2 Customizing the Excel Interface   156

39.3 Troubleshooting Common Issues   156

39.4 Excel Best Practices   156

39.5 Staying Updated with Excel 2023   157

Chapter 40: Conclusion   158

40.1 Review of Key Concepts   158

40.2 Resources for Further Learning   159

40.3 Excel Certification Options   159

40.4 The Future of Excel   159

40.5 Final Thoughts   160

Excel 2023 Shortcut Cheat Sheet   161

New Features   168

Additional Resources for Excel Mastery   169

Appendix   170

Excel 2023 Function Reference Guide   170

1. Text Functions   170

2. Logical Functions   171

3. Date and Time Functions   172

4. Lookup and Reference Functions   172

5. Mathematical Functions   173

6.VStack and HStack Functions   174

7. TextSplit and TextBefore Functions   174

Introduction to Excel 2023

Microsoft Excel 2023 is a powerful spreadsheet software application developed by Microsoft, and it is one of the most widely used tools for data analysis, calculation, visualization, and reporting. Excel has been a fundamental tool for businesses, educators, researchers, and individuals for several decades, and with each new version, it continues to evolve and offer more features and functionalities to meet the diverse needs of its users.

Why Use Excel 2023 ?

Excel 2023 offers a plethora of benefits that make it an indispensable tool in various domains:

1. Data Organization: Excel provides a structured grid-like interface, enabling users to organize data in rows and columns efficiently. This tabular layout makes it easy to store, manage, and manipulate vast amounts of information.

2. Data Analysis: Excel offers a wide range of built-in formulas and functions that allow users to perform complex calculations, analyze data, and generate insights quickly. From basic arith-

metic to advanced statistical functions, Excel can handle diverse analytical tasks.

3. Data Visualization: Visual representation of data is crucial for understanding patterns and trends. Excel 2023 enables users to create a variety of charts and graphs, helping to communicate information effectively.

4. Automation: Excel allows users to automate repetitive tasks using macros and Visual Basic for Applications (VBA). This feature saves time and reduces the chance of errors when dealing with repetitive operations.

5. Integration with Other Applications: Excel seamlessly integrates with other Microsoft Office applications like Word and PowerPoint. It also supports importing and exporting data from various file formats and databases.

6. Collaboration: Excel 2023 enhances collaboration by enabling real-time co-authoring and sharing through Microsoft's cloud-based platform, OneDrive. Multiple users can work on the same spreadsheet simultaneously.

7. Conditional Formatting: Excel's conditional formatting feature allows users to apply different formats to cells based on specific criteria, making it easier to identify patterns and outliers.

8. PivotTables: PivotTables offer an advanced way to summarize and analyze large datasets quickly. Users can slice and dice data, perform aggregations, and create interactive reports.

9. What-If Analysis: Excel's scenario manager and goal seek tools enable users to perform what-if analysis, allowing them to explore different scenarios and understand the impact of changes in data.

10. Customization: Excel 2023 allows users to customize their workbooks, create custom formulas, design templates, and develop user-defined functions to suit specific requirements.

Whether you are a student, business professional, researcher, or hobbyist, Excel 2023 provides a versatile platform for data management and analysis. Understanding its capabilities and mastering its features can significantly enhance your productivity and decision-making processes.

1.1. What is Excel 2023?

Excel 2023 is the latest version of Microsoft Excel, a powerful and widely used spreadsheet software application. It is a part of the Microsoft Office suite and is designed to help users perform a variety of tasks, ranging from simple calculations to complex data analysis and visualization. Excel 2023 comes with several enhancements and new features, building upon the functionality of previous versions, making it even more efficient and user-friendly.

1.2. Installing Excel 2023

To install Excel 2023, follow these steps:

Step 1: Purchase Microsoft Office 2023 - You can buy it from the official Microsoft website or authorized retailers.

Step 2: Download the Installer - After purchasing, log in

to your Microsoft account, and download the Office 2023 installer.

Step 3: Run the Installer - Locate the downloaded file and run the installer. Follow the on-screen instructions to install Excel 2023.

Step 4: Activation - Once the installation is complete, open Excel 2023 and sign in with your Microsoft account to activate the software.

1.3. Understanding the Excel Interface

The Excel 2023 interface is designed to provide an intuitive user experience. Here are the key elements:

1. **Ribbon**: Located at the top, it contains various tabs, each with related commands organized into groups.
2. **Worksheet Area**: The main grid where you enter and manipulate data. It consists of columns (labeled with letters) and rows (labeled with numbers).
3. **Formula Bar**: Displays the content of the active cell and allows you to enter or edit data and formulas.
4. **Name Box**: Shows the cell reference of the active cell. You can also use it to define and navigate to named ranges.
5. **Quick Access Toolbar**: Contains frequently used commands like Save, Undo, and Redo.
6. **Status Bar**: Displays information about the current mode, calculations, and other helpful indicators.

1.4. Basic Excel Terminology

1. **Cell**: The intersection point of a row and a column on a worksheet grid, used to store data.
2. **Workbook**: A file that contains one or more worksheets.
3. **Worksheet**: A single sheet within a workbook where you can enter and manipulate data.
4. **Formula**: An equation used to perform calculations and produce results based on cell references and mathematical operations.
5. **Function**: A predefined formula that performs specific calculations, such as SUM, AVERAGE, and COUNT.
6. **Chart**: A visual representation of data using graphs and charts.

1.5. Setting Up Your First Spreadsheet

Setting up your first spreadsheet in Excel is a fundamental step to begin working with the software. Here's a step-by-step guide to creating a simple spreadsheet:

Step 1: Open Excel: Launch Microsoft Excel 2023 by clicking on its icon in the Start menu or by searching for it in the search bar.

Step 2: Choose a Blank Workbook: After Excel opens, you'll see a list of templates. For our first spreadsheet, select "Blank Workbook" to start with a new, empty spreadsheet.

Step 3: Understanding the Interface: Familiarize yourself with the Excel interface, as explained in the previous section.

You will see the Ribbon, Quick Access Toolbar, Formula Bar, Worksheet Area, Name Box, Sheet Tabs, and Status Bar.

Step 4: Enter Data: In cell A1 (the first cell of the worksheet), type "Product," and in cell B1, type "Price." These will be our column headers.

Step 5: Enter Sample Data: In cells A2 and A3, enter a few sample product names (e.g., "Item 1" and "Item 2"). In cells B2 and B3, enter corresponding prices (e.g., "10" and "15"). Your spreadsheet should look like this:

A	B
———-	————
Product	Price
Item 1	10
Item 2	15

Step 6: AutoFill: To complete the data for more products and prices quickly, click on cell A3 (which contains "Item 2"). Move the mouse cursor to the bottom-right corner of the cell until it turns into a small square (the fill handle). Click, hold, and drag the fill handle down to fill cells A4, A5, and so on with product names. Excel will automatically increment the numbers for you.

Step 7: Add More Data: Complete the product names for a few more items in column A and their respective prices in column B.

Step 8: Basic Calculation: In cell C2, type the formula to

calculate the total price for "Item 1." Type "=B2*1.15" (without quotes) and press Enter. This formula multiplies the price in cell B2 by 1.15 (15% markup) to calculate the total price.

Step 9: AutoFill the Formula: Click on cell C2 (which contains the formula), then use the fill handle to drag it down to fill the formula for all products in column C. Excel will automatically adjust the cell references for each product.

Step 10: Formatting: Select cells A1 to C1 to highlight the column headers. Go to the "Home" tab on the Ribbon and apply formatting options like bolding, changing font size, or changing cell background color to make the headers stand out.

Step 11: Save Your Spreadsheet: Click on the "File" tab in the top-left corner, then select "Save As." Choose a location on your computer, provide a filename, and click "Save."

Congratulations! You've set up your first spreadsheet in Excel 2023.

Interactive Exercises

Exercise: Install Excel 2023 and create a simple spreadsheet with basic formatting. **Question**: What are the key differences between Excel 2023 and previous versions, and how can you navigate the Excel 2023 interface?

Chapter 2: Navigating the Excel Interface

Understanding and getting comfortable with Excel's interface is a critical first step to becoming proficient in this versatile application. The interface consists of several key components that facilitate a range of functions, from data entry and calculation to advanced analysis and visual presentation. This chapter focuses on five main components of the Excel interface: the Ribbon, Quick Access Toolbar, Views, customization features, and the Help system.

2.1. Understanding the Ribbon

The Ribbon, situated at the top of your Excel screen, is the primary tool that you use to interact with Excel. It holds an extensive set of commands grouped into tabs based on their function, such as Home, Insert, Page Layout, Formulas, Data, Review, and View. Each tab contains groups of related commands. For example, the Home tab includes the Clipboard, Font, Alignment, Number, Styles, Cells, and Editing groups.

Clicking on a tab will reveal its associated tools and options. Some groups have a small arrow at the bottom right of the group that you can click to see more options related to that group.

This arrow is called the Dialog Box Launcher. For example, clicking on the arrow in the Font group in the Home tab will open a dialog box with more font options.

Understanding the Ribbon is fundamental to becoming proficient in Excel. By exploring the tabs and groups, you can familiarize yourself with the commands available to you and learn where to locate the tools you need.

2.2. Working with the Quick Access Toolbar

Just above the Ribbon, you'll find the Quick Access Toolbar. This toolbar is designed to provide easy access to commands you use frequently. By default, it includes the Save, Undo, and Redo commands, but you can customize it to include any command you want.

To add a command, right-click on any command in the Ribbon and select 'Add to Quick Access Toolbar.' This feature can be a real time-saver because it keeps your most frequently used commands right at your fingertips, regardless of which Ribbon tab you're working in.

2.3. Managing Views

Excel provides several ways to view your worksheets, depending on what you're trying to achieve. The main views are Normal, Page Layout, and Page Break Preview, each accessible from the 'View' tab on the Ribbon.

- The Normal view is the default view for Excel and is likely the one you use most often. It is ideal for data input and writing formulas.

- Page Layout view shows how your worksheet will appear on the printed page. It's useful when preparing your sheet for printing or for working with headers and footers.

- Page Break Preview lets you adjust where the page breaks will be when the worksheet is printed. It's an excellent tool for ensuring that your printed data is well organized and easy to read.

By learning how to navigate and use these different views, you can make your work in Excel more efficient and effective.

2.4. Customizing the Excel Environment

Excel offers numerous ways to customize its environment to better suit your workflow. You can customize the Ribbon by adding your own tabs with commands you frequently use. Right-click the Ribbon, select 'Customize the Ribbon,' then 'New Tab' to create your own tab and fill it with your chosen commands.

Excel also lets you adjust general settings through the Excel Options dialog box, accessible from the 'File' tab. Here, you can modify settings related to formulas, proofing, saving, language, advanced options, and more.

Customizing your Excel environment can make your work more comfortable and help you complete tasks more efficiently by arranging the tools in the way that best suits you.

2.5. Using Help Features

Finally, Excel's Help features are invaluable for new and experienced users alike. The 'Tell me what you want to do' search box at the top of the Ribbon is a great place to start. By typing in a keyword or phrase, Excel will suggest related commands.

For more in-depth help, go to the 'Help' tab on the Ribbon. Here, you can access Microsoft's extensive online resources, including tutorials, videos, forums, and more. There is also an option to contact Microsoft Support for more personalized assistance.

In conclusion, mastering the Excel interface is about understanding the role of each component and how they can assist you in your tasks. As you become more comfortable with the Ribbon, Quick Access Toolbar, various views, customization features, and the Help system, you'll find that your efficiency and productivity in Excel will greatly increase.

Interactive Exercises

- **Exercise**: Customize the Excel environment by modifying the Ribbon and Quick Access Toolbar.
- **Question**: How can you manage different views in Excel, and what are the benefits of customizing the Excel environment?

Chapter 3: Creating and Saving Workbooks

Chapter 3: Creating and Saving Workbooks

Working with Excel starts with understanding the basics of creating and saving workbooks, using templates, and managing your saved files. This chapter will provide a comprehensive exploration of these topics, laying the groundwork for efficient use of Excel.

3.1. Creating New Workbooks

A workbook is essentially a file containing one or more related worksheets, allowing you to organize various kinds of related information. Creating a new workbook in Excel is straightforward. You can go to 'File' on the Ribbon, select 'New', and then 'Blank Workbook'. This action will create a fresh, untitled workbook, ready for you to input data.

When creating a new workbook, you'll usually begin with a single worksheet. However, you can add more worksheets according to your needs by clicking on the '+' icon next to the existing worksheet tabs at the bottom.

3.2. Saving and Opening Workbooks

Once you have entered your data into a workbook, you need to save it for future reference or modification. Click on 'File', and then 'Save As', to choose a location on your computer where the file will be stored. Excel will prompt you to name the file, giving you a chance to label your work appropriately. Excel files typically have an .xlsx extension, although other formats are available based on your needs.

To open a saved workbook, you can navigate to 'File' and then 'Open'. Excel allows you to browse your files and choose the workbook you want to open. You can also open recent workbooks quickly via the 'Recent' tab under 'Open'.

3.3. Using Templates

Excel offers a range of pre-built templates, providing a significant time-saving tool and ensuring consistency across documents. To use a template, go to 'File', then 'New', and you can explore a variety of templates, such as budget planners, calendars, invoices, and more. Once you've found a template that suits your needs, select it and click 'Create'. Excel will generate a new workbook based on your chosen template.

Templates can be a great starting point, especially for complex tasks that have a standard structure, as they provide a professionally designed, customizable format.

3.4. AutoRecover and AutoSave

Excel has built-in features to protect your work in the event of a crash or power failure: AutoRecover and AutoSave. AutoRecover automatically saves a backup copy of your workbook at regular intervals, which can be adjusted in the Excel options. This feature allows you to recover your work if something unexpected occurs before you've had a chance to save your workbook.

AutoSave, which is available if you are a Microsoft 365 subscriber and are saving to OneDrive or SharePoint, saves your workbook automatically as you work, ensuring that your changes are saved in real-time.

These features provide peace of mind, minimizing the risk of losing significant amounts of work due to unexpected events.

3.5. Importing and Exporting Data

Excel provides robust options for importing data from a wide range of sources, including other Excel workbooks, CSV files, databases, and the web. This feature allows you to bring in data from various places and consolidate it within your workbook for analysis.

To import data, go to the 'Data' tab on the Ribbon, and select 'Get Data'. Excel will guide you through the steps to import the data, depending on the source.

Similarly, you can export data from Excel to various formats. This capability allows you to share your findings in a suitable format, whether that be another Excel file, a PDF for presentation purposes, or a CSV file for use in another software.

Understanding these fundamental processes of creating and

saving workbooks, using templates, recovering and autosaving work, and importing and exporting data is crucial in Excel. These skills form the foundation for your work in Excel, allowing you to focus more on data analysis and less on managing the workbooks.

Interactive Exercises

Exercise: Create a new workbook using a template, save it in different formats, and explore Auto Recover features.

Question: What are the various ways to create and save workbooks, and how can you import and export data in Excel?

Chapter 4: Entering and Editing Data

After you've become familiar with the Excel interface and workbook management, the next step is to learn about entering and editing data. This chapter will provide a comprehensive guide on how to input data, edit cell contents, use the AutoFill feature, and manipulate cells, rows, and columns. We'll also cover how to copy and move data within your worksheets.

4.1. Inputting Data

Entering data into an Excel worksheet is straightforward. Simply select a cell by clicking on it and then start typing. Press 'Enter' when you're done to input the data into the cell. Excel is versatile in terms of the types of data it can handle, including text, numbers, dates, times, and more.

For example, you might input a list of products sold by your company. You would select cell A1, type the first product name, press 'Enter', and then continue with the rest of your products. Excel will store each entry in the respective cell, allowing for further data manipulation and analysis later.

4.2. Editing Cell Contents

Editing cell contents in Excel is also easy. To edit data in a cell, you can double-click the cell and then make your changes, or you can select the cell and press F2. The contents of the cell will be highlighted, and you can change the existing data or add to it. Press 'Enter' when you're done to save the changes.

For instance, if you've made a typo in your product list, you can simply navigate to the cell with the typo, double-click, correct the typo, and then press 'Enter' to save the correction.

4.3. Using AutoFill

Excel's AutoFill feature can save you significant time when you need to fill cells with a pattern or a series. This could be a series of numbers, dates, months, etc. Simply enter the initial value(s) in your cells, select the cell(s), move your cursor to the bottom right corner until it turns into a plus sign, and then click and drag down or across to fill the remaining cells.

For example, if you want to fill a column with consecutive dates, you can type the first date in cell A1, use the AutoFill handle to drag down, and Excel will automatically fill in the subsequent dates.

4.4. Inserting and Deleting Cells, Rows, and Columns

There may be times when you need to insert or delete cells, rows, or columns in your worksheet. To insert a cell, right-click on a cell, and choose 'Insert' from the dropdown menu. Excel will then ask whether you want to shift the existing cells down or to the right. To delete a cell, right-click on it and select

17

'Delete'. Similar steps apply when inserting or deleting rows or columns.

Let's say you forgot to include a product in your list. You can easily add it by right-clicking on the row where you want the product name to go, selecting 'Insert', and then typing the product name in the new row.

4.5. Copying and Moving Data

Excel also makes it simple to copy and move data within your workbook. To copy data, select the cell or range of cells, right-click, and choose 'Copy', or simply press Ctrl+C. Then click on the cell where you want to place the copied data, right-click, and select 'Paste', or press Ctrl+V.

To move data, select the cell or range of cells, right-click, and select 'Cut', or press Ctrl+X. Then right-click on the cell where you want to move the data to and select 'Paste', or press Ctrl+V.

Suppose you have sales data in columns B and C, but you want the data in columns D and E instead. You can select columns B and C, cut the data, select column D, and then paste the data. Excel will move your data to the new location without changing anything.

In conclusion, becoming proficient in entering and editing data is a key part of working with Excel. Mastering these functions will allow you to efficiently manage and manipulate your data, paving the way for effective data analysis.

Interactive Exercises

Exercise: Input and edit data in a worksheet, use AutoFill, and practice inserting, deleting, copying, and moving cells. **Question**: How can you efficiently enter and edit data, and what are the methods for managing cells, rows, and columns?

Chapter 5: Working with Cells and Ranges

Microsoft Excel's functional design revolves around the manipulation of cells and ranges, which form the basic building blocks of any spreadsheet. This chapter focuses on fundamental operations, such as selecting, formatting, aligning, and splitting cells, and the use of styles and themes, which all contribute to the efficiency, accuracy, and visual appeal of your data presentation.

5.1. Selecting Cells and Ranges

The first step in manipulating data in Excel is understanding how to select cells. A single click on any cell makes it the active cell, ready for data entry or formatting. For ranges, which are sets of two or more cells, click and drag your mouse across the desired area to select it. Ranges can span across rows and columns, encompassing large sets of data.

Selecting entire rows or columns is another vital skill. By clicking on the row number or column letter, you can select the entire row or column. This feature is useful when applying formatting changes across a wide range of cells, deleting content, or inserting additional rows or columns.

For more complex tasks, you might need to select non-contiguous cells or ranges. This can be accomplished by holding down the Ctrl key and clicking each desired cell or range. For those times when you need to work with all the data in a worksheet, Excel allows you to select all cells by pressing Ctrl+A or clicking on the small rectangle at the intersection of the row numbers and column letters.

5.2. Formatting Cells and Ranges

Once you've selected a cell or a range, Excel offers a wide array of formatting options that can be accessed by right-clicking and selecting 'Format Cells'. This opens a dialog box offering a host of options across multiple tabs, including number, alignment, font, border, fill, and protection.

For example, the 'Number' tab allows you to specify the type of data the cell holds. You can select options like 'General', 'Number', 'Currency', 'Accounting', 'Date', 'Time', and more. Each category has additional settings to refine the data presentation. For instance, you could specify the number of decimal places, the date format, whether to use a thousand separator, and more.

5.3. Using Styles and Themes

The use of styles and themes can dramatically improve the appearance of your workbooks and provides consistency across worksheets. Styles are a set of formatting options that can be applied all at once to a cell or range, controlling aspects such as font, color, and number formatting.

Themes, on the other hand, apply to the entire workbook and

include a coordinated set of fonts, colors, and effects. Themes are especially useful when you're creating reports or presentations and need a consistent, professional look. For instance, you might choose a theme that matches your company's colors and use this across all your business spreadsheets for a consistent, professional look.

5.4. Cell Alignment and Text Wrapping

Cell alignment and text wrapping provide additional control over how your data is presented. Excel offers options to align text vertically (top, center, bottom) and horizontally (left, center, right) within the cell. This is especially useful when dealing with cells of varying sizes, as you can ensure that your data is presented consistently.

Text wrapping is a handy feature for cells containing more text than can be displayed in the cell's current width. With text wrapping enabled, instead of the text overflowing into adjacent cells or being cut off, Excel increases the cell's height to accommodate all the text, effectively making the text appear on multiple lines within the cell.

5.5. Merging and Splitting Cells

Excel provides options to merge multiple cells into one larger cell, a useful tool for creating distinct headers or for when you need to center a title across a particular range. The 'Merge & Center' command on the 'Home' tab combines the selected cells into one and centers the text within.

Conversely, if you have a merged cell that you need to split back into its original, individual cells, you can use the 'Unmerge

Cells' command. It's important to note that when you unmerge cells, only the content from the top-left cell of the merged range will be preserved; the rest will be discarded.

With a solid understanding of these key concepts and practices, you can start to unlock Excel's full potential. It's through mastering these granular controls that you can create effective, well-organized, and visually appealing spreadsheets, whether for business analysis, project management, academic research, or personal finance tracking.

Interactive Exercises

Exercise: Select and format cells, apply styles and themes, align text, and merge and split cells. **Question**: How can you enhance the appearance of cells and ranges, and what are the options for text alignment and cell merging?

Chapter 6: Managing Worksheets and Workbooks

When working with Excel, your projects often evolve into complex arrays of data spread across multiple worksheets within a workbook. This chapter focuses on advanced worksheet and workbook management techniques such as adding, deleting, renaming, and moving worksheets, as well as grouping, hiding, and linking them.

6.1. Adding and Deleting Worksheets

In any given Excel workbook, you begin with a single default worksheet. As you add more data and your project becomes more complex, you may need to add additional worksheets. To do this, you'll find the '+' icon next to your existing worksheet tabs at the bottom of your Excel interface. Clicking this will automatically generate a new, blank worksheet, with a default title of 'SheetX', where 'X' refers to the chronological order of the sheet creation.

Conversely, if a worksheet becomes unnecessary or if you need to declutter your workbook, deleting a worksheet is just as simple. Right-clicking on the respective worksheet tab will reveal a dropdown menu with a 'Delete' option. However, it's crucial to remember that this operation cannot be undone and will result in the permanent loss of all data within that worksheet.

6.2. Renaming and Moving Worksheets

Default worksheet names ('Sheet1', 'Sheet2', etc.) are often insufficient for understanding the content of each sheet. Therefore, renaming worksheets to more accurately represent their content is a good practice. This can be done by right-clicking the worksheet tab, selecting 'Rename', and then typing in a new, descriptive name. For example, if your workbook includes monthly sales data, appropriate names might be 'January Sales', 'February Sales', and so on.

As your workbook expands, rearranging your worksheets may become necessary. Excel allows you to move worksheets by clicking and dragging the worksheet tab to its desired place. This enables you to logically order your worksheets for easier navigation, whether it's chronologically, alphabetically, or in order of importance.

6.3. Grouping and Ungrouping Worksheets

When you're working with multiple worksheets that require similar data or formatting, Excel's grouping feature becomes incredibly handy. To group worksheets, you select the first sheet, then hold down the Ctrl key and click each additional sheet you want to include in the group.

Once your worksheets are grouped, any action you perform is applied to all sheets in the group. For instance, if you change the font size in one cell, the change will apply to the corresponding cell in all grouped worksheets. Remember to ungroup your sheets after you've made your changes to avoid unintentionally modifying all sheets.

6.4. Hiding and Unhiding Worksheets

Excel gives you the option to hide worksheets, which can be useful for reducing clutter in your workbook or protecting sensitive information. This can be done by right-clicking the worksheet tab and selecting 'Hide' from the dropdown menu.

The hidden worksheets are not deleted; they are just out of sight. To access a hidden worksheet, you can right-click any worksheet tab, select 'Unhide', and a dialog box will open allowing you to choose which hidden sheet to reveal.

6.5. Linking Worksheets

One of Excel's powerful features is the ability to create dynamic links between cells in different worksheets. These links create a relationship such that a change in one cell automatically reflects in another. To create a link, you'll start by selecting the cell where you want to display the linked data, type '=', navigate to the desired cell in a different worksheet, and then press 'Enter'.

For instance, if you're tracking monthly sales figures across several worksheets, you might create a 'Summary' sheet that links to the total from each month's sheet. When you update the monthly totals, the 'Summary' sheet will automatically reflect these changes, ensuring your data remains consistent and up-to-date across your workbook.

In conclusion, understanding how to manage worksheets and workbooks in Excel is vital for maintaining an organized and efficient working environment. As your projects grow and evolve, these skills will help ensure your data remains accessible, comprehensible, and easy to navigate, allowing you to focus on analyzing your data rather than managing it.

Interactive Exercises

- **Exercise**: Add, delete, rename, move, group, ungroup, hide, and unhide worksheets, and practice linking between them.
- **Question**: What are the techniques for managing worksheets, and how can you effectively organize and link them?

Case Study: Inventory Management for a Small Retail Business

- **Scenario**: A small retail business uses Excel to manage its inventory, tracking products across multiple locations.
- **Application**: Demonstrate how to add, delete, rename, move, group, and link worksheets to manage different product categories and locations.
- **Outcome**: Improved inventory tracking, streamlined ordering process, and enhanced decision-making.

Chapter 7: Basic Formulas and Functions

Formulas and functions are the bedrock of Excel, they provide the ability to perform calculations, manipulate data, and carry out complex operations.

7.1. Understanding Formulas

Excel formulas are expressions that perform operations on data. They can do basic arithmetic operations, such as addition, subtraction, multiplication, and division, but they can also perform complex operations by using functions.

A simple formula might look like "=A1+A2", which would add together the values in cells A1 and A2. This formula can be extended to include more complex calculations, such as "=A1+A2*A3", which would multiply the value in A2 by the value in A3, and then add the result to the value in A1.

Excel follows the order of operations (parentheses, exponents, multiplication and division, addition and subtraction) when calculating formulas. To change the order of operations, you can use parentheses. For example, in the formula above, if you wanted to add A1 and A2 together before multiplying the result by A3, you would use the formula "=(A1+A2)*A3".

7.2. Using Basic Functions

Functions are predefined formulas that perform calculations using specific values, called arguments, in a particular order, or structure. Functions can be used to perform simple or complex calculations.

There are over 400 functions available in Excel, some of the basic ones include:

- SUM: Sum a group of numbers.
- AVERAGE: Calculate the mean of a group of numbers.
- COUNT: Count the number of cells in a range that contain numbers.
- MIN: Find the smallest number in a group of numbers.
- MAX: Find the largest number in a group of numbers.

7.3. Relative and Absolute Cell References

Cell references are a critical aspect of Excel formulas. A cell reference refers to the address of a cell in a worksheet. The two main types of cell references are relative and absolute.

- Relative cell references automatically change when a formula is copied and pasted to another cell. For example, if a formula in cell B1 references cell A1 and you copy the formula to cell B2, the formula will change to reference cell A2. This is useful when you want to apply the same calculation to multiple rows or columns.
- Absolute cell references remain constant, regardless of where they are copied. They are denoted by a dollar sign before the column letter and/or the row number (e.g., A1,

$A1, A$1). For example, if a formula in cell B1 references cell A1 and you copy the formula to cell B2, the formula will still reference cell A1. This is useful when you want to refer to a cell that contains a constant value or formula.

7.4. Using the Formula Auditing Tools

The Formula Auditing group on the Formulas tab contains tools that help with auditing and debugging formulas.

- The Trace Precedents tool shows arrows that point from the cells providing input to the formula in the selected cell.
- The Trace Dependents tool shows arrows that point to the cells that depend on the value in the selected cell.
- The Remove Arrows tool removes all arrows drawn by the Trace Precedents and Trace Dependents tools.
- The Show Formulas tool toggles the display of formulas in the worksheet. When it's turned on, all cell formulas are displayed in the worksheet rather than the results of the formulas.

7.5. Troubleshooting Formulas

Excel provides several tools to help identify and fix errors in formulas.

- The Error Checking tool checks the worksheet for common errors. If it finds a potential error, it displays an error message. You can then choose to edit the formula or ignore the error.
- The Evaluate Formula tool allows you to see the order in

which a formula is calculated.

- The Watch Window tool is a pane that you can display to monitor the values of multiple cells at the same time.

When a formula can't be calculated, Excel displays an error value in the cell. The error value begins with a pound sign (#) and is followed by an error name, such as #VALUE!, #REF!, #DIV/0!, #NAME?, #NUM!, #NULL!, or #N/A.

Interactive Exercises

Exercise: Create simple formulas, use basic functions, and understand relative and absolute cell references. **Question**: How do you construct and troubleshoot formulas, and what are the differences between relative and absolute references?

Chapter 8: Advanced Formulas and Functions

Advanced formulas and functions allow you to manipulate and analyze complex data.

8.1. Using Logical Functions

Logical functions return a value of TRUE or FALSE based on a logical test. The main logical functions include:

- IF: Performs a test and returns one value if the test is true and another value if the test is false.
- AND: Returns TRUE if all arguments are true; returns FALSE if any argument is false.
- OR: Returns TRUE if any argument is true; returns FALSE if all arguments are false.
- NOT: Returns the opposite of a logical value - NOT(TRUE) returns FALSE; NOT(FALSE) returns TRUE.

8.2. Using Lookup Functions

Lookup functions search for a value in a data list or table and return a corresponding value.

- VLOOKUP: Searches for a value in the leftmost column of a table and returns a value in the same row from a specified column. The "V" in VLOOKUP stands for "vertical".
- HLOOKUP: Similar to VLOOKUP, but searches for a value in the top row of a table and returns a value in the same column from a specified row. The "H" in HLOOKUP stands for "horizontal".

8.3. Using Date and Time Functions

Excel has several functions that work with dates and times.

- NOW: Returns the current date and time.
- TODAY: Returns the current date.
- DATE: Returns the date given a year, month, and day.
- TIME: Returns the time given an hour, minute, and second.
- DAY: Returns the day of the month from a date.
- MONTH: Returns the month from a date.
- YEAR: Returns the year from a date.
- HOUR: Returns the hour from a time.
- MINUTE: Returns the minute from a time.
- SECOND: Returns the second from a time.

8.4. Using Text Functions

Text functions work with text values, also known as strings.

- LEFT: Returns a specified number of characters from the start of a string.
- RIGHT: Returns a specified number of characters from the end of a string.
- MID: Returns a specified number of characters from the middle of a string.
- LEN: Returns the number of characters in a string.
- FIND, SEARCH: Return the position of a specific string of characters within a string.
- REPLACE, SUBSTITUTE: Replace specific text within a string.

8.5. Using Array Formulas

Array formulas perform operations on multiple values rather than a single value. They can perform calculations on rows, columns, or an entire range.

For example, the array formula "{=SUM(A1:A3*B1:B3)}" multiplies each element in the range A1:A3 by the corresponding element in the range B1:B3, and then sums the results.

You enter an array formula by pressing Ctrl+Shift+Enter, rather than just Enter. When you do this, Excel encloses the formula in curly braces {}, indicating that it's an array formula.

Interactive Exercises

Exercise: Explore logical, lookup, date and time, text, and array formulas. **Question**: How can you utilize advanced functions to perform complex calculations, and what are some practical applications?

Chapter 9: Working with Tables

Tables in Excel are a structured way to group and manage related data. They allow for efficient organization, data analysis, and overall enhancement of data visibility. Tables are not just data containers; they provide a range of features that can increase your productivity

9.1. Creating Tables

To create a table in Excel, you first need to select the range of cells that your table will encompass. This range should include the data you want in the table as well as the headers for your columns. Once you've selected your range, navigate to the 'Insert' tab on the ribbon at the top of Excel and click 'Table'. This will open a dialogue box which prompts you to confirm the range for your table and to specify whether your table has headers. Click 'OK', and Excel will create your table.

Creating tables in Excel has several key benefits:

- They make your data easier to manage. Once your data is in a table, you can use the sort and filter options in the header row to manage your data effectively.
- They are more visually appealing and make your data easier

to understand. Excel automatically applies a basic style to your table, but you can choose from a variety of other styles to tailor the look of your table to your needs.

- They automatically resize as you add or remove data. If you type data into a cell adjacent to a table, Excel will automatically incorporate it into the table.

For example, let's say you have a range of data in cells A1 through D20, including headers. To create a table, you would highlight the cells A1 to D20, click 'Insert', then click 'Table'. Excel will create a table for your specified range and apply a default table style.

9.2. Formatting Tables

Once your table is created, you can change its formatting using Excel's built-in table styles. These styles adjust the color and font used in your table and include several components such as a header row, total row, banded rows, and the first column.

To format a table, click on any cell within the table. This will activate the 'Table Tools' option on the ribbon, under which you'll find the 'Design' tab. Click on 'Design' to view all available table styles. You can hover over any style to preview it on your table, and simply click to apply it.

You can also specify the table style elements you want to include. Do you want banded rows or banded columns? Would you like a special style for the first column? You can choose your preferences in the 'Table Style Options' group in the 'Design' tab. For example, you might choose a style that includes banded rows to make your data easier to read.

9.3. Sorting and Filtering Tables

Sorting and filtering are two key features of Excel tables. They allow you to control the display of your data so you can focus on specific parts of your data set.

Sorting data in an Excel table is as easy as clicking on the drop-down arrow next to a column header and choosing your preferred sort option. For instance, if you have a column of sales data, you can sort it in ascending or descending order to easily see the lowest and highest values.

Filtering data can help you focus on specific entries in your table. Just like sorting, you can filter data by clicking on the drop-down arrow next to a column header. From here, you can check or uncheck boxes to filter data based on your requirements. For example, you might want to filter a table to only show entries from a certain region or time period.

9.4. Using Table References in Formulas

When you create a table in Excel, the program automatically assigns it a name. By default, the first table you create in a workbook is named 'Table1', the second is 'Table2', and so on. You can see and change this name in the 'Table Name' box on the 'Table Design' tab.

Excel allows you to use this table name in your formulas. This makes your formulas easier to understand because you can see which table the data is coming from. For example, if your table is named 'Sales' and you have a column labeled 'Profit', you can find the total profit with a formula like "=SUM(Sales[Profit])". This formula adds up all the values in the 'Profit' column of the 'Sales' table.

9.5. Converting Tables to Ranges

Sometimes, you may want to convert a table back to a standard range of cells. You might do this if you want to remove the table features but keep the data and formatting. To convert a table to a range, click anywhere in the table to activate the 'Table Tools' tab. Go to the 'Design' tab, and in the 'Tools' group, click 'Convert to Range'. Excel will ask you to confirm. Click 'Yes', and your table will be converted to a range, removing features such as the header row filter arrows.

Working with tables can greatly enhance your data analysis capabilities in Excel. The features available in tables can help you manage large sets of data, making tasks such as sorting, filtering, and analyzing data much simpler and more efficient.

Interactive Exercises

Exercise: Create and format tables, sort and filter them, and use table references in formulas. **Question**: What are the benefits of using tables in Excel, and how can you manipulate them for data analysis?

Chapter 10: Data Validation and Conditional Formatting

Data validation and conditional formatting are two powerful tools in Excel that help maintain data integrity and enhance data visualization.

10.1. Applying Data Validation

Data validation in Excel allows you to set certain restrictions on what kind of data can be entered into a cell. This can be a helpful way to maintain consistency and accuracy of data, particularly when multiple users are entering data in the same workbook.

To apply data validation to a cell or range of cells, select the cells, then click on the 'Data' tab on the ribbon. In the 'Data Tools' group, click 'Data Validation'. This will open the Data Validation dialog box, where you can set your data validation criteria.

Excel offers several types of data validation, including:

- Whole number: The cell can only contain whole numbers within a specified range.
- Decimal: The cell can only contain decimal numbers within

a specified range.

- List: The cell can only contain a value from a predefined list.
- Date: The cell can only contain dates within a specified range.
- Time: The cell can only contain times within a specified range.
- Text length: The cell can only contain text of a certain length.
- Custom: You can create a custom validation rule using a formula.

For example, to restrict a cell to whole numbers between 1 and 100, you would select 'Whole number' from the 'Allow' box, 'between' from the 'Data' box, and then type 1 and 100 in the 'Minimum' and 'Maximum' boxes respectively.

10.2. Creating Drop-Down Lists

Drop-down lists can be created using data validation. A drop-down list restricts the data that can be entered into a cell to a predefined set of values.

To create a drop-down list, select the cell where you want the list, click the 'Data' tab on the ribbon, click 'Data Validation', and then select 'List' from the 'Allow' box. In the 'Source' box, enter the values for the list, separated by commas.

For example, if you want to create a drop-down list of fruit names in cell A1, you would select cell A1, open the Data Validation dialog box, select 'List' from the 'Allow' box, and then enter "Apple, Banana, Cherry" in the 'Source' box.

10.3. Using Conditional Formatting

Conditional formatting in Excel allows you to automatically change the formatting of cells based on their contents. For example, you might want to highlight cells that contain values above a certain threshold, or color-code cells based on their value.

To apply conditional formatting, select the cells you want to format, click the 'Home' tab on the ribbon, and then click 'Conditional Formatting'. Excel provides several types of conditional formatting, including:

- Highlight Cells Rules: These rules change the fill color, font color, or other formatting options of cells that meet certain conditions, such as being greater than a certain number, containing certain text, or having a certain date.
- Top/Bottom Rules: These rules format the top or bottom numbers or percentages of cells, or cells that are above or below average.
- Data Bars: These rules fill cells with gradient or solid fill that represents the value of the cell compared to other cells.
- Color Scales: These rules color cells based on their value, with a gradient of two or three colors.
- Icon Sets: These rules assign an icon to cells based on their value.

10.4. Managing Conditional Formatting Rules

Once you have applied conditional formatting, you can manage your rules using the Conditional Formatting Rules Manager. This dialog box allows you to see all the conditional formatting rules applied to the selected cells or the entire worksheet.

You can access the Conditional Formatting Rules Manager by clicking the 'Home' tab on the ribbon, then clicking 'Conditional Formatting', and finally selecting 'Manage Rules'.

From here, you can create new rules, edit existing rules, delete rules, and change the order in which the rules are applied. The order of rules is important because if a cell meets the criteria for more than one rule, only the first rule will be applied.

10.5. Highlighting Cells with Conditional Formatting

You can use conditional formatting to highlight cells or rows that meet certain criteria. For example, you could highlight all sales totals that exceed a certain amount, or highlight dates that are in the past.

To highlight cells, select the cells you want to format, click the 'Home' tab on the ribbon, click 'Conditional Formatting', and then choose a rule. You can choose from the built-in rules, or you can create a new rule that specifies exactly what criteria to use and how to format the cells.

For example, to highlight sales totals in column B that exceed $5000, you would select column B, open the Conditional Formatting menu, select 'Highlight Cells Rules', then 'Greater Than'. In the dialog box, enter 5000 and choose a formatting style. Click 'OK', and all cells in column B that contain a value greater than 5000 will be highlighted.

By using data validation and conditional formatting, you can increase the accuracy of data entry and enhance the visualization of your data, making it easier to analyze and interpret.

Interactive Exercises

Exercise: Apply data validation rules, create drop-down lists, and use conditional formatting to highlight cells. **Question**: How can data validation and conditional formatting enhance data integrity and visualization?

Chapter 11: Working with Charts

Spreadsheets are useful for organizing and calculating data, but visualizing that data is often where the real insights happen. In Excel, one of the most powerful tools for data visualization is the chart. In this chapter, we will delve into the fundamentals of creating and customizing charts in Excel, before progressing to more advanced techniques.

11.1 Creating Charts

Excel offers a multitude of chart types, each designed to best represent a particular kind of data set. From simple bar or line charts that show trends over time, to more complex scatter plots that can indicate correlations between different variables, there's almost no end to the types of stories you can tell with charts in Excel.

Creating a chart is straightforward:

1. First, select the data you want to plot in your chart. Excel is smart enough to use the labels from your first row and column as the x and y axes of your chart, so make sure to include these in your selection.

2. With your data selected, go to the 'Insert' tab on the Ribbon. You'll see a 'Charts' group which contains all the chart types Excel offers.

3. Choose a chart type that suits your data and what you want to convey. Upon clicking, Excel automatically generates a chart.

For example, if you have a set of data that displays sales numbers for the past twelve months, a line chart would be an excellent way to visualize the trend in sales over the course of a year.

11.2 Formatting Charts

After creating a chart, you'll likely need to make some adjustments to ensure it looks the way you want and presents the data in the clearest manner. Excel gives you myriad options to change the look and feel of your chart.

Once you click on a chart, Excel brings up the 'Chart Tools' on the Ribbon, which includes 'Design' and 'Format' tabs:

1. Under the 'Design' tab, you'll find options to select a quick layout that changes the layout of your chart or pick a chart style that alters the color and effect of your chart. Here, you can also change your chart type, switch data over the axis, or even select a different data source.

2. In the 'Format' tab, you'll find tools that allow you to fine-tune the chart elements. You can change the fill color, outline, or effects of any element in the chart, including the chart area, plot area, data series, and labels. You can also modify the text in your chart, changing the font, font size, or font color.

11.3 Modifying Chart Elements

Excel charts are made up of several components, such as the chart title, data labels, legend, axes, and more. You can add, remove, or modify these elements to suit your needs.

For example, to add a title to your chart, go to the 'Design' tab under 'Chart Tools'. Click on 'Add Chart Element', then 'Chart Title', and decide where you want to place the title. Now, click on the title box in your chart and type the desired title.

11.4 Creating Combination Charts

Combination charts are unique in that they allow you to plot different types of data sets that might have different scales and units, all on the same chart. It's like having multiple charts, but layered on top of one another.

Creating a combination chart involves a few steps:

1. First, create a standard chart with all your data.

2. Click on the data series you want to change, right-click, and choose 'Change Series Chart Type'.

3. In the Change Chart Type dialog box, select a new chart type for the data series and click OK.

For instance, if you wanted to show the correlation between advertising spend and sales volume over a year, you could use a combination chart. The primary vertical axis could show the advertising spend, and the secondary vertical axis could represent sales volume.

11.5 Creating Sparklines

Sparklines are tiny, word-sized graphics that can be placed wherever you have some space in your Excel worksheet. They're great for showing trends in a series of values, such as seasonal increases or decreases, economic cycles, or highlighting maximum and minimum values.

Here's how you create a sparkline:

1. Organize your data in rows or columns. You might have a column for each month of the year and a row for each product you're tracking, for example.

2. Select an empty cell where you want to insert the sparkline (this is usually next to the data you're visualizing).

3. Go to the 'Insert' tab on the Ribbon, click on 'Sparklines' in the 'Sparklines' group, and then choose the type of sparkline you want (Line, Column, or Win/Loss).

4. In the 'Create Sparklines' dialog box that appears, specify the data range for your sparkline, and click OK.

Visualizing data with charts is more of an art than a science, and it requires practice and experience to do well. It's about choosing the right chart type, formatting it in a way that's easy to understand, and then refining it so that it tells a compelling story.

Interactive Exercises

Exercise: Create and format various types of charts, modify elements, and create sparklines. **Question**: What are the different types of charts available in Excel, and how can you customize them to represent data effectively?

Chapter 12: Advanced Charting Techniques

The power of Excel extends beyond basic data analysis to incorporate sophisticated charting capabilities. This chapter delves into advanced charting techniques in Excel, including PivotCharts, the Quick Analysis tool, and various statistical and hierarchical charts.

12.1 Creating PivotCharts

PivotCharts are an extension of PivotTables, offering a visual representation of your PivotTable data. Because PivotCharts are directly linked to PivotTables, any adjustments you make in the PivotTable, like filtering or changing the layout, are instantly reflected in the PivotChart.

To create a PivotChart:

1. Click anywhere within your PivotTable to activate the 'PivotTable Tools' on the Ribbon.
2. Go to the 'Analyze' (or 'Options') tab.
3. Click 'PivotChart' in the 'Tools' group.
4. In the 'Insert Chart' dialog box, select the chart type and sub-type you wish to use, and then click 'OK'.

It's important to note that while PivotCharts offer dynamic visual analysis capabilities, their complexity may make them more suitable for advanced users or those comfortable navigating PivotTables.

12.2 Using the Quick Analysis Tool

Excel's Quick Analysis tool provides swift access to many of Excel's powerful data analysis features. Upon selecting a cell range, the Quick Analysis button becomes visible at the bottom-right of the selection. Clicking this button brings up several analysis options, such as formatting, charts, totals, tables, and Sparklines.

The Quick Analysis tool is particularly handy when working with large datasets as it offers a streamlined way to visualize and draw insights from the data without requiring detailed knowledge of Excel's deeper features.

12.3 Creating Histograms and Box and Whisker Charts

Histograms and Box and Whisker charts offer statistical representations of your data.

A Histogram displays frequency data, showing how often different data points occur. It's useful for visualizing data distributions, spotting outliers, and identifying skewness in your data.

The Box and Whisker chart provides a graphical rendition of the minimum, first quartile, median, third quartile, and maximum of a dataset. The "box" represents the interquartile range where 50% of the data points lie, and the "whiskers" represent the spread of the rest of the data.

51

To create either of these charts, go to the 'Insert' tab on the Ribbon, click on 'Insert Statistic Chart', and select 'Histogram' or 'Box and Whisker' accordingly.

12.4 Creating Treemap and Sunburst Charts

Treemap and Sunburst charts offer visually engaging ways to represent hierarchical data.

A Treemap chart is ideal for comparing proportions within a hierarchy. Each level of the hierarchy is represented by a colored rectangle (or 'branch'), which is then further divided into smaller rectangles ('leaves').

A Sunburst chart, on the other hand, provides a hierarchical view of your data in a radial format. It's beneficial when you want to show how one ring is broken into its contributing pieces.

Both charts are under the 'Insert Hierarchy Chart' in the 'Charts' group on the 'Insert' tab.

12.5 Creating Waterfall and Funnel Charts

Waterfall and Funnel charts are useful for different types of sequential data representation.

A Waterfall chart is excellent for understanding the cumulative effect of sequentially introduced positive or negative values. These can be initial and final values, and the intermediate steps are vertical bars—creating a 'waterfall' effect.

Conversely, a Funnel chart displays values across multiple stages in a process. The chart's shape is determined by the values in each stage, making it useful for displaying data that reduces over time, like a sales pipeline or a website conversion funnel.

Both types can be created via the 'Insert Waterfall or Stock Chart' dropdown in the 'Charts' group on the 'Insert' tab.

These advanced charting techniques are designed to facilitate deeper data analysis and clearer data presentation. However, the power of these charts comes with increased complexity, so a solid understanding of Excel basics is recommended before diving into these features.

Interactive Exercises

Exercise: Create PivotCharts, histograms, box and whisker, treemap, sunburst, waterfall, and funnel charts. **Question**: How can advanced charting techniques provide deeper insights into data, and what are the steps to create them?

Chapter 13: Working with PivotTables

PivotTables are among the most sophisticated and powerful features offered by Excel, enabling users to summarize, analyze, explore, and present data in an understandable and organized manner. Regardless of your dataset's size, PivotTables can help you turn data-filled cells into meaningful information. This chapter will guide you through the process of creating, modifying, and enhancing PivotTables, and even delve into more advanced features, such as calculated fields and items.

13.1 Creating PivotTables: The Power of Summarized Data

A PivotTable provides a way to extract significance from a sea of numbers and present it in an easily digestible format. Let's explore the process of creating a PivotTable.

1. Click on a cell in your dataset.
2. Navigate to the 'Insert' tab in the Ribbon, and within the 'Tables' group, select 'PivotTable'.
3. The 'Create PivotTable' dialog box will appear. Confirm that the data range in the 'Select a table or range' field matches your intended dataset.

4. Next, decide whether you want the PivotTable to appear in a new worksheet or an existing one. Once decided, click 'OK'.

5. You will be taken to your chosen sheet, where you can set up your PivotTable in the PivotTable Field List by dragging and dropping fields to the desired areas.

Keep in mind that numeric data, or the values you wish to analyze, typically go into the 'Values' area. In contrast, non-numeric data, or the categories you wish to analyze your values by, usually go into 'Rows' or 'Columns'.

13.2 Modifying PivotTables: Customizing Your Data View

PivotTables are not static – they can be tailored and adjusted to fit your needs precisely. You can easily add or remove fields, rearrange the order of fields, apply filters to focus on specific information, and even change the summary function (from sum to average, for instance) for a field.

To access these options, simply click on any cell within the PivotTable. This will display the 'PivotTable Field List', where you can make adjustments to fit your specific requirements.

13.3 Using Slicers and Timelines: Simplifying Data Filtering

While PivotTables offer significant data summarizing power, Slicers and Timelines take this a step further by providing visual methods to filter the data in a PivotTable.

Slicers allow you to filter your data by simply selecting from a list of options. Adding a Slicer to a PivotTable involves the following steps:

1. Click any cell within the PivotTable.
2. Under the 'PivotTable Analyze' tab (or 'Options' tab in some Excel versions) in the Ribbon, select 'Insert Slicer'.
3. The 'Insert Slicers' dialog box will appear, allowing you to choose which fields to create Slicers for.

Timelines, similar to Slicers, provide a visual way to filter data. However, Timelines are specifically designed for date fields, allowing users to filter data across different time periods. You can add a Timeline to your PivotTable by selecting 'Insert Timeline' instead of 'Insert Slicer'.

13.4 Creating Calculated Fields and Items: Enhancing Your PivotTable

Calculated Fields and Items offer an added layer of customization to your PivotTables. They allow you to create new fields or items based on calculations derived from existing data.

A Calculated Field lets you generate new fields in your PivotTable, computed from an expression that you define. The expression can involve existing numeric fields in the PivotTable.

To add a Calculated Field:

1. Click anywhere in the PivotTable to display the PivotTable Field List.
2. In the 'PivotTable Analyze' (or 'Options') tab, click on 'Fields, Items & Sets', then choose 'Calculated Field'.

On the other hand, a Calculated Item lets you create new items within an existing field. These new items are computed from an expression you define, which can involve existing items within the same field.

13.5 Creating PivotTables from Multiple Ranges: Connecting Data

Excel also supports the creation of PivotTables from multiple data ranges through the use of the 'Data Model' feature. The Data Model allows you to create relationships between different tables (data ranges), which can then be analyzed together in a PivotTable.

1. Format your data ranges as 'Tables' by clicking anywhere within a data range, then selecting 'Table' under the 'Insert' tab.
2. Once your Tables are prepared, go to the 'Insert' tab and select 'PivotTable'.
3. In the 'Create PivotTable' dialog box, choose 'Use this workbook's Data Model', select the location for your PivotTable, and click 'OK'.
4. In the PivotTable Field List, you'll now see all the Tables present in the Data Model. You can add fields from any

Table to your PivotTable.

PivotTables are a transformative feature of Excel that can bring clarity to complex datasets, allowing you to identify trends and patterns that might otherwise remain hidden. As you become more proficient with PivotTables, you'll find that they offer a wide range of possibilities for customizing and understanding your data.

Interactive Exercises

Exercise: Create and modify PivotTables, use slicers and timelines, create calculated fields and items, and connect multiple data ranges. **Question**: How do PivotTables summarize data, and what are the ways to customize and enhance PivotTables?

Case Study: Sales Analysis for a Tech Company

- **Scenario**: A tech company uses PivotTables to analyze sales data, identifying trends and opportunities.
- **Application**: Show how to create and modify PivotTables to summarize sales by region, product, and salesperson.
- **Outcome**: Increased sales efficiency, targeted marketing efforts, and better alignment with customer needs.

Chapter 14: Advanced PivotTable Techniques

PivotTables are more than just a summarizing tool. They can also be used to create dynamic and interactive reports, thanks to the wide array of advanced features Excel provides. In this chapter, we'll examine some of these features, such as Power Pivot, Data Analysis Expressions (DAX), the Data Model, table relationships, and hierarchies in PivotTables.

14.1 Using Power Pivot: Extending Your Data Analysis

Power Pivot is an Excel add-in that allows you to manage and analyze large datasets. It extends the capabilities of PivotTables by allowing you to import data from multiple sources, create relationships between tables, and create advanced calculations using DAX.

To use Power Pivot, you'll first need to enable the add-in:

1. Click on 'File' in the Ribbon, then 'Options'.
2. In the 'Excel Options' dialog box, click on 'Add-Ins'.
3. At the bottom of the dialog box, in the 'Manage' dropdown,

select 'COM Add-ins', then click 'Go'.

4. In the 'COM Add-Ins' dialog box, check the 'Microsoft Office Power Pivot' box, then click 'OK'.

Once enabled, you'll see a new 'Power Pivot' tab in the Ribbon, from where you can manage your data model and perform advanced data analysis tasks.

14.2 Creating Measures with DAX: Elevating Calculations

DAX (Data Analysis Expressions) is a formula language designed specifically for Power Pivot and Power BI. It allows you to create calculated columns and measures (calculations you add to a PivotTable).

Measures are calculations performed on data in the model rather than at the row level. They are used in the 'Values' area of a PivotTable and are calculated based on the current context set by any associated row labels, column labels, report filters, or slicers.

To create a measure:

1. Click anywhere in your PivotTable.
2. Go to the 'Power Pivot' tab in the Ribbon, then select 'Measures' and 'New Measure'.
3. In the 'New Measure' dialog box, specify the 'Table name' where the measure will be stored, the 'Measure name', the 'Formula', and the 'Number format', then click 'OK'.

14.3 Using the Data Model: Unifying Data Sources

The Data Model is an integral part of Excel's advanced data analysis features. It allows you to combine data from different tables, providing a unified view for reporting and analysis. When you create relationships between tables in the Data Model, you can analyze related data without needing to combine everything into a single table.

When you import data into Power Pivot, it is automatically added to the Data Model. You can also add existing Excel tables to the Data Model by selecting any cell in the table, then going to the 'Power Pivot' tab and selecting 'Add to Data Model'.

14.4 Creating Relationships Between Tables: Linking Your Data

In the Data Model, you can create relationships between tables, much like in a relational database. This allows you to use fields from different tables in your analyses as if they were from a single table.

To create a relationship:

1. Go to the 'Power Pivot' tab in the Ribbon, then select 'Manage'.
2. In the Power Pivot window, select 'Diagram View'.
3. Drag the field from one table to the related field in another table.

The relationship is represented by a line connecting the two tables. Excel will use this relationship when analyzing data across the tables.

14.5 Using Hierarchies in PivotTables: Structuring Your Data

Hierarchies provide a way to group related fields together, making it easier to navigate large PivotTables. A hierarchy is a list of fields from the same table, arranged so that each field provides detail about the field above it.

To create a hierarchy:

1. Go to the 'Power Pivot' tab in the Ribbon, then select 'Manage'.
2. In the Power Pivot window, select 'Diagram View'.
3. In the table where you want to create a hierarchy, right-click on the field that will be at the top of the hierarchy, then select 'Create Hierarchy'. Name the hierarchy as desired.
4. To add more fields to the hierarchy, drag them onto the hierarchy name.

In your PivotTable, you can now use the hierarchy as a unified field, which expands to show the individual fields when you click on the '+' icon next to the hierarchy name.

Interactive Exercises

Exercise: Explore Power Pivot, create measures with DAX, unify data sources, link tables, and use hierarchies. **Question**: How can advanced PivotTable techniques extend data analysis, and what are the applications of DAX and data relationships?

Chapter 15: Introduction to Power Query

In the realm of data analysis, the value of clean, well-structured data is unparalleled. Microsoft's Power Query for Excel is a revolutionary tool designed to ease the process of data discovery, connection, combination, and refining. Power Query provides a wide array of features, allowing users to delve into data cleaning and structuring with precision and efficiency. In this chapter, we take an in-depth look into the world of Power Query, exploring its vast potential in handling data.

15.1 Understanding Power Query: Bridging the Gap Between Data and Insight

Power Query, in essence, is a data connection technology that allows users to streamline the process of accessing, combining, and refining data across a myriad of sources. This tool, integrated into Excel, provides a consistent and user-friendly interface for data transformation tasks, empowering users to build advanced data preparation solutions.

What sets Power Query apart is its ability to automate data cleaning tasks. Users can execute a series of data transformations, all of which Power Query remembers. When the same data connection is refreshed, or the process is applied to a new data set, Power Query automatically carries out these steps, turning a previously tedious task into a simple, one-click process.

15.2 Importing Data with Power Query: Simplifying Data Access

Power Query significantly expands the range of data sources accessible within Excel. From traditional databases, such as SQL Server, MySQL, Oracle, to files like Excel workbooks, CSV and XML, SharePoint lists, Salesforce reports, Azure tables, and web pages, Power Query enables seamless and straightforward data importing.

The process for importing data is intuitive:

1. Navigate to the 'Data' tab on the Ribbon and select 'Get Data'.
2. Depending on your source, you make the appropriate selection in the drop-down menu.
3. Locate your file or enter the necessary server information, then proceed with the 'Import'.
4. Power Query opens a new window, showcasing your imported data, and offering a range of options to clean and transform the data before it is loaded into Excel.

15.3 Cleaning and Transforming Data with Power Query: Unleashing Data's True Potential

The true power of Power Query lies in its robust data transformation capabilities. With the data imported, Power Query offers a myriad of tools to clean and structure your data. Users can eliminate unnecessary columns or rows, alter data types, partition columns, extract or replace values, and so much more.

Importantly, Power Query records every transformation applied to the data. These recorded steps form a script that is executed every time the data connection is refreshed. This automation dramatically reduces the time and effort spent on data cleaning and preparation.

15.4 Merging and Appending Queries: Streamlining Your Data Structure

Beyond data cleaning, Power Query provides the tools to merge or append datasets, crafting precisely the data structure required for your analyses.

The 'Merge' function in Power Query is akin to joining tables in a database. It allows you to bring together two tables based on a common column, enabling a holistic view of your data.

On the other hand, the 'Append' function stacks one dataset atop another. When dealing with two or more tables with identical columns, you can stack them to form a comprehensive, unified dataset.

15.5 Loading Queries to the Workbook: Completing the Data Preparation Journey

Once you've finished with the data importing, transformation, and restructuring, the final step is loading your refined data into your Excel workbook.

Power Query provides two primary options to load your query:

1. 'Load To' allows you to specify where your data should be placed. You can opt to create a new table in a new or existing worksheet, or create only a connection for further use.
2. 'Close & Load' automatically loads your data as a new table into a new worksheet.

With Power Query at your disposal, the process of data preparation becomes efficient and straightforward. The flexibility and power of this tool enable you to transform raw, disordered data into a well-structured and clean format, ready for insightful analysis. By mastering Power Query, you're not just preparing data; you're paving the road to valuable insights.

Interactive Exercises

Exercise: Understand Power Query, import data, clean and transform data, merge and append queries, and load queries to the workbook. **Question**: What is Power Query, and how does it bridge the gap between data and insight in Excel?

Chapter 16: Advanced Power Query Techniques

Power Query is a dynamic tool that allows Excel users to streamline their data analysis process. While the basic functionalities offer considerable power, Power Query also packs a range of advanced features that provide even more control and flexibility over your data. This chapter will delve into the more sophisticated aspects of Power Query, including using the Query Editor, creating calculated and conditional columns, grouping and aggregating data, and employing parameters in queries.

16.1 Using the Query Editor

At the heart of Power Query is the Query Editor, a space where you can manipulate, transform, and clean data. Upon connecting with a data source, Power Query loads the data into the Query Editor, offering a bird's eye view of the dataset. The interface provides numerous options for data manipulation, including filtering and sorting columns, changing data types, splitting columns, merging queries, and so much more.

Crucially, the Query Editor tracks each action taken within the Applied Steps pane. These steps form a script of transformations applied to the data, repeated each time the data connection refreshes. This feature automates repetitive data cleaning tasks, freeing up time for valuable analysis.

16.2 Creating Calculated Columns

Power Query facilitates the creation of calculated columns, which are new columns formed through a formula referencing existing columns. These calculated columns are generated during the data load process, with the results stored in the data model for future use. To create a calculated column, select the 'Add Column' tab within the Query Editor and choose the 'Custom Column' option. A dialog box will appear, where you can define the formula for the calculated column.

16.3 Using Conditional Columns

In addition to calculated columns, Power Query enables the creation of conditional columns. A conditional column's value for each row is determined by a set of predefined conditions. For instance, you could generate a conditional column that categorizes another column's value, tagging it as 'High' if over 100, and 'Low' otherwise. The creation process mirrors that of calculated columns: select the 'Add Column' tab within the Query Editor and choose the 'Conditional Column' option.

16.4 Grouping and Aggregating Data

When working with large data sets, it's often useful to group related data. Power Query supports data grouping and offers a host of aggregation functions, including sum, count, average, minimum, maximum, and more. In the Query Editor, select the 'Transform' tab and choose the 'Group By' option. This will prompt a dialog box, allowing you to specify the column(s) for grouping and the type of aggregation function to apply.

16.5 Using Parameters in Queries

To enhance the flexibility and dynamism of your queries, Power Query supports the use of parameters. Parameters serve as placeholders for values used repeatedly within your query. For example, a date parameter can be employed in a query step to filter data. Whenever the date needs to be changed, updating the parameter value will adjust the query accordingly. You can create a parameter by navigating to the 'Home' tab in the Query Editor and selecting 'Manage Parameters'.

By diving into these advanced techniques, you will discover the immense capabilities of Power Query, harnessing its potential to simplify and elevate your data analysis process. Power Query serves as a testament to Excel's power as a data analysis tool, further bridging the gap between raw data and valuable insights.

Interactive Exercises

Exercise: Use the Query Editor, create calculated and conditional columns, group and aggregate data, and use parameters in queries. **Question**: How can advanced Power Query techniques streamline data structure and enhance data analysis?

Chapter 17: Introduction to Power BI

In the information age, data analysis has emerged as a crucial aspect of business management. With an ocean of data at our fingertips, the ability to extract meaningful insights can offer a competitive edge. Power BI, a suite of business analytics tools developed by Microsoft, offers comprehensive solutions for data analysis. With its robust, user-friendly features, Power BI can transform raw data into valuable insights, presenting data in an interactive, visually engaging format. In this chapter, we will immerse ourselves in the world of Power BI, exploring its various functionalities from data importation to the creation of dynamic dashboards.

17.1 Understanding Power BI: Redefining Data Analysis

Power BI is a versatile collection of apps, connectors, and software services that collaborate to convert a multitude of data sources into coherent, visually immersive, and interactive insights. It caters to various data sources, from Excel workbooks and on-premises SQL Server databases to different cloud services, facilitating seamless data connectivity and visualization.

The primary components of Power BI include:

1. Power BI Desktop: This Windows desktop application provides a powerful report creation environment, where data queries, data modeling, and report layouts take shape.
2. Power BI Service: Also known as Power BI online, this cloud-based service is where reports from Power BI Desktop are published and shared.
3. Power BI Mobile: These are Power BI applications available on Windows, iOS, and Android devices, enabling access to data and reports from anywhere.

17.2 Importing Data into Power BI: Laying the Groundwork

The journey of data analysis begins with data importation. Power BI's capabilities extend to numerous data sources, from simple Excel spreadsheets and complex SQL Server databases to various cloud services. Upon connection, Power BI pulls in the data, placing it into a data model ready for manipulation, analysis, and visualization. The imported data tables are accessible from the Fields pane, providing a clear overview of your data structure.

17.3 Creating Reports in Power BI: Translating Data into Insights

Reports in Power BI offer a comprehensive perspective into datasets, enabling a multi-dimensional view that presents diverse insights in an interactive format. Reports can contain a single visualization or multiple pages teeming with various visuals. Each visual within a report offers an interactive way to present data, enabling viewers to explore data layers, discover

71

patterns, and derive insights.

Creating a report involves dragging and dropping fields onto a report canvas, where Power BI automatically generates a visual based on the data. The flexibility of Power BI allows you to modify these visuals to suit your presentation needs better.

17.4 Publishing to the Power BI Service: Propagating Insights

Power BI Desktop serves as the creation hub for reports, but it is through the Power BI Service that these reports reach a wider audience. Upon crafting a report in Power BI Desktop, you can publish it to the Power BI Service. This cloud-based platform not only allows others to view and interact with the report but also facilitates collaboration on shared data, report sharing, and dashboard creation, which collectively enhance the reach and impact of your data analysis.

17.5 Creating Dashboards in Power BI: Weaving a Data Story

A dashboard in Power BI is a consolidated presentation platform that employs visuals, reports, and other data elements to narrate a data story. Given its single-page design, a well-crafted dashboard incorporates only the most vital elements of the story. The process of creating a dashboard involves pinning visualizations, reports, and other data elements to the dashboard, where they appear as tiles. The dashboard continuously updates, reflecting real-time changes in data, providing an always-current snapshot of your data narrative.

By diving into the advanced capabilities of Power BI, you're equipping yourself with a powerful tool that can elevate your data analysis and decision-making processes, effectively transforming raw, disconnected data into meaningful, actionable insights.

Interactive Exercises

Exercise: Understand Power BI, import data, create reports, publish to the Power BI service, and create dashboards. **Question**: How does Power BI redefine data analysis, and what are the steps to translate data into insights?

Chapter 18: Collaborating in Excel

In an era where business decisions are heavily data-driven, the ability to collaborate effectively on data analysis tasks is crucial. Microsoft Excel, renowned for its comprehensive spreadsheet functionalities, offers a suite of tools designed to facilitate seamless collaboration. This chapter will delve deeper into Excel's collaborative capabilities, including sharing and co-authoring workbooks, implementing protection measures for workbooks and worksheets, tracking changes for audit trails, and utilizing comments for meaningful discussions and feedback within the team.

18.1 Sharing Workbooks: Elevating Teamwork

The traditional method of sharing an Excel workbook—emailing it as an attachment—was often fraught with difficulties such as version inconsistencies and inefficiencies in collaboration. With the advent of cloud technology, Excel has revamped its sharing functionalities. Workbooks can now be shared directly from within Excel to cloud platforms like OneDrive or SharePoint. This allows multiple users to access the workbook simultaneously, enabling real-time collaboration and eliminating version conflicts. The 'Share' button, conveniently located at the top right of the Excel interface, is your gateway to efficient teamwork.

18.2 Co-Authoring Workbooks: Harnessing Collective Wisdom

Co-authoring is a transformative feature that complements the sharing functionality of Excel. It allows multiple users to access and edit a workbook concurrently, fostering a truly collaborative work environment. When a workbook is hosted on OneDrive or SharePoint, team members can simultaneously work on the document. You can even view other users' cursors moving as they make edits in real time, promoting transparency and synergy among the team. Moreover, team members can engage in discussions right within Excel, using the comments feature to facilitate communication.

18.3 Protecting Workbooks and Worksheets: Balancing Collaboration with Control

While collaboration is essential, data protection is equally crucial. Excel offers robust features that allow you to control editing permissions at the workbook and worksheet levels. You can lock an entire workbook to prevent structural changes such as adding or deleting worksheets. Alternatively, you can protect specific worksheets and designate certain cells that can be edited. Excel also supports advanced security options, including password protection and permissions for specific users to edit ranges within a protected worksheet. This balance of collaborative freedom and control safeguards your data while fostering a productive work environment.

18.4 Tracking Changes: Maintaining Accountability and Transparency

Tracking changes in Excel allows you to keep tabs on who made edits and what those edits entail. This is invaluable in a collaborative setting, as it provides a detailed audit trail and enhances accountability. Upon activating the 'Track Changes' feature, Excel will highlight cells with modifications, allowing you to see exactly what was changed, who made the change, and when. This ensures that each team member's contribution is visible and traceable, enhancing accountability and transparency within the team.

18.5 Adding and Reviewing Comments: Streamlining Communication

Comments serve as a medium for adding notes, posing questions, or providing feedback directly linked to specific cells within a worksheet. They enable clear, concise, and context-specific communication among team members. Adding a comment is as simple as right-clicking a cell and selecting 'New Comment.' These comments are accessible to everyone with access to the workbook, facilitating a dynamic exchange of ideas. Moreover, comments can be replied to, resolved, or deleted, supporting effective communication threads. In co-authoring scenarios, the comment function can serve as a chat box for real-time discussions.

Excel's collaboration features not only promote efficiency and productivity but also ensure data security and transparency. By leveraging these tools, teams can work synergistically, transforming individual inputs into collective insights. With

Excel, collaboration is not just about working together—it's about working smarter.

Interactive Exercises

Exercise: Share and co-author workbooks, protect them, track changes, and add and review comments. **Question**: How can Excel elevate teamwork, and what are the ways to balance collaboration with control?

Chapter 19: Automating Tasks with Macros

The digital revolution has brought forth an era where automation is pivotal in driving efficiency and accuracy across numerous fields. In the realm of data analysis and spreadsheet management, Microsoft Excel emerges as a powerful tool, especially with its feature of macros—a set of pre-defined instructions that automate repetitive tasks. This chapter delves deeper into the intricacies of Excel macros, guiding you through the process of understanding, recording, running, editing macros, and introduces you to Visual Basic for Applications (VBA), the programming language that powers macros in Excel.

19.1 Understanding Macros: The Backbone of Excel Automation

At their core, macros in Excel are sequences of commands or instructions bundled together as a single entity to perform a task automatically. They can be as straightforward as a command instructing Excel to apply specific formatting to a range of cells, or as complex as a series of commands for carrying out advanced data manipulation and analysis. Macros are particularly useful when you need to execute a series of tasks repeatedly. By executing pre-recorded steps, macros can save a significant amount of time, reduce manual intervention, and minimize potential human errors.

19.2 Recording Macros: Documenting Steps for Future Repetition

Excel provides a user-friendly feature to create macros, called the "Record Macro" tool. This tool works much like a video camera, recording every action you make in Excel to replay them in the future. To record a macro, you simply navigate to the Developer tab and select the Record Macro button. Then you proceed with the tasks that you want the macro to replicate. Once finished, you click on the Stop Recording button. Excel then translates these steps into VBA code, which can be viewed and edited if needed.

19.3 Running and Editing Macros: Effortless Execution and Modification

Once a macro has been created, it's time to put it into action. Running a macro involves a few simple clicks: select the Macros button in the Developer tab, choose the macro you wish to run from the list, and click Run. As the macro runs, it performs the set of instructions recorded earlier, automating the task effortlessly.

But what if the recorded macro needs adjustments? What if the task evolves, and the macro needs to evolve with it? Excel enables you to modify the macro's code. You can access the macro's VBA code, where you can alter the recorded instructions or add new ones, ensuring that your macro remains relevant and useful.

19.4 Understanding VBA: The Driving Force of Excel Macros

Visual Basic for Applications, known commonly as VBA, is the programming language that fuels Excel macros. Part of the Microsoft Office suite of applications, VBA enables users to automate a myriad of tasks within these applications. VBA, while powerful, is designed to be accessible. Users who are comfortable with Excel's interface often find it easier to understand VBA's syntax and structure. Having a grasp of VBA can significantly boost your ability to create complex macros that automate a wide range of tasks in Excel.

19.5 Creating Macros with VBA: Tailoring Automation to Your Needs

While recording a macro is quite straightforward and efficient for automating simple tasks, there might be situations where you need to create macros to handle more complex tasks. This is where writing VBA scripts comes into play. By scripting in VBA within the VBA editor, you can create macros that provide greater flexibility and control over Excel's functionalities. These macros can execute complex tasks, like performing loops over ranges of cells or making conditional decisions based on cell content. VBA may seem daunting at first, but numerous resources are available to guide beginners and help them grasp the basics of VBA.

In conclusion, Excel macros, with their ability to automate repetitive tasks and improve accuracy, are a boon to any individual or team working extensively with Excel. Whether you're a novice learning to record basic macros or an advanced user creating complex macros with VBA, the potential to streamline processes and enhance productivity is immense. Embark on your journey of mastering Excel macros and discover the true power of automation.

Interactive Exercises

Exercise: Understand, record, run, and edit macros, and create macros with VBA. **Question**: What is the role of macros and VBA in Excel automation, and how can they be tailored to specific needs?

Chapter 20: Excel for Financial Analysis

Financial analysis is an essential function in business decision-making. It provides a basis for making strategic financial decisions, assessing a company's financial health, and forecasting future financial performance. A tool of choice for financial analysis is Microsoft Excel, recognized for its robust computational and analytical capabilities. This chapter delves into the ways Excel can be utilized for financial analysis, including employing financial functions, crafting financial models, performing 'what-if' analysis, leveraging the Analysis ToolPak, and generating amortization schedules.

20.1 Using Financial Functions

Financial functions are pre-built formulas in Excel designed to execute specific financial calculations. They are organized into categories such as interest rates, investments, loans, and depreciation, offering a toolbox of options to conduct financial analysis. Excel's financial functions can handle complex calculations, making it a powerful tool in financial analysis. For instance, functions like PMT, FV, and NPV facilitate computations related to loan payments, future value of investments, and net present value of cash flows. These functions can streamline the financial analysis process, providing fast and accurate results.

20.2 Building Financial Models

Financial models are simplified, abstract representations of financial situations. They allow analysts to make forecasts, analyze potential investment opportunities, and make informed financial decisions. Excel, with its wide range of features and functionalities, is perfectly suited for building such financial models. It offers tools like pivot tables for summarizing data, data validation for maintaining data integrity, and a variety of financial functions for performing financial computations. These features empower users to construct robust financial models that can handle complex scenarios and manage variable inputs.

20.3 Performing What-If Analysis

What-If Analysis is a technique used in Excel to change the values in cells and analyze how these changes impact the outcome of formulas on the worksheet. It's essentially about exploring various financial scenarios and understanding potential outcomes. Excel provides multiple tools for performing what-if analysis, including data tables for displaying a range of outcomes in a table format, scenario manager for comparing various scenarios, and Goal Seek for finding the required input to achieve a defined goal. These tools enable users to evaluate different scenarios and make optimal financial decisions.

20.4 Using the Analysis ToolPak

The Analysis ToolPak is an Excel add-in that extends the program's capabilities by providing additional financial and statistical functions. These functions enable more advanced data analysis without requiring complex formulas or custom VBA code. Some features the Analysis ToolPak offers include tools for creating histograms, generating random numbers, and performing analysis of variance (ANOVA). By enabling the Analysis ToolPak, users can enhance their Excel environment, making complex financial analyses more manageable and straightforward.

20.5 Creating Amortization Schedules

Amortization schedules are detailed tables of periodic loan payments, showing the breakdown of each payment into principal and interest components. These schedules provide a clear picture of how the loan will be repaid over time. Excel, with its array of date and financial functions, is an ideal platform for creating amortization schedules. By using functions like PMT for calculating total payment, IPMT for calculating interest payment, and PPMT for calculating principal payment, users can build comprehensive amortization schedules for any loan.

Mastering Excel's capabilities for financial analysis can significantly enhance your ability to make informed financial decisions, evaluate financial health, and gain valuable insights into your organization's financial standing.

Interactive Exercises

Exercise: Use financial functions, build financial models, perform what-if analysis, use the Analysis ToolPak, and create amortization schedules. **Question**: How can Excel support financial analysis, and what are the key tools and functions for financial modeling?

Case Study: Financial Planning for a Startup

- **Scenario**: A startup uses Excel for financial planning, including budgeting, forecasting, and investment analysis.
- **Application**: Demonstrate how to use financial functions, build financial models, and perform what-if analysis.
- **Outcome**: Effective financial planning, risk mitigation, and strategic investment decisions.

Chapter 21: Excel for Statistical Analysis

Statistical analysis is fundamental to data interpretation and decision-making in numerous fields. Microsoft Excel, with its extensive features, offers a versatile platform for such analysis. This chapter unravels Excel's capability for statistical analysis, shedding light on the use of its various statistical functions, performing descriptive and inferential statistics, conducting regression analysis, and creating probability distributions.

21.1 Using Statistical Functions

Excel's statistical functions are a comprehensive set of tools designed to perform a variety of statistical calculations. They cover a broad range of categories, including functions for determining central tendency, variability, distribution shape, and relationships between variables. The functions range from the simple AVERAGE function for calculating the mean of a dataset to more complex functions like CORREL for calculating the correlation between two datasets. By making use of these functions, users can perform intricate statistical analyses without needing to understand the underlying calculations.

21.2 Analyzing Data with Descriptive Statistics

Descriptive statistics provide a way to summarize and understand large datasets by providing measures of central tendency, dispersion, and skewness. Excel offers a multitude of functions to perform descriptive statistics, like AVERAGE, MEDIAN, and MODE for measuring central tendency, and STDEV, VAR, and RANGE for measuring dispersion. Additionally, Excel's Data Analysis add-in provides a Descriptive Statistics tool that can calculate these measures and more for a dataset at the click of a button.

21.3 Testing Hypotheses with Inferential Statistics

Inferential statistics allow us to make inferences about a population based on a sample of data. Excel provides tools to perform a variety of hypothesis tests, such as t-tests, ANOVA, and chi-square tests. These tests can help determine if differences or relationships observed in your sample data are statistically significant. By performing these tests in Excel, users can confidently make inferences about their data and support their decisions with statistical evidence.

21.4 Performing Regression Analysis

Regression analysis is a powerful statistical analysis technique used to understand the relationship between variables. Excel's Data Analysis add-in provides a Regression tool that allows you to perform linear regression analysis. This tool provides a comprehensive output that includes the regression equation, R-squared values, and significance tests for the overall model and individual predictors. With this information, users can interpret the output and make predictions based on their regression model.

21.5 Creating Probability Distributions

Probability distributions are fundamental to statistical analysis, providing a description of how the values of a random variable are distributed. Excel provides a variety of functions to create and analyze different probability distributions, including normal, binomial, and Poisson distributions. By using these functions and Excel's charting capabilities, users can visualize and analyze these distributions, enhancing their understanding of their data.

In conclusion, Excel, with its vast array of statistical functions and tools, makes statistical analysis accessible and practical. From simple descriptive statistics to complex inferential tests and regression analysis, Excel empowers users to derive meaningful insights from their data and make data-driven decisions.

Interactive Exercises

Exercise: Use statistical functions, analyze data with descriptive statistics, test hypotheses, perform regression analysis, and create probability distributions. **Question**: How can Excel facilitate statistical analysis, and what are the methods for descriptive and inferential statistics?

Chapter 22: Excel for Data Science

In the realm of data, data science emerges as the process of extracting insights and knowledge from massive amounts of structured and unstructured data. At the core of this process is Microsoft Excel, a tool celebrated for its analytical and data manipulation capabilities. This chapter provides an in-depth exploration of the role of Excel in data science, including understanding the data science process, cleaning and preparing data, exploratory data analysis, predictive model building, and data visualization.

22.1 Understanding the Data Science Process

The data science process comprises a sequence of stages that facilitate the systematic extraction of insights from data. These stages span data collection, data cleaning and preparation, exploratory data analysis, model building, evaluation, and the communication of results. Each stage is critical to the overall process, and Excel provides an array of functionalities that enable these stages. For example, Excel's data import capabilities facilitate data collection, while its functions and formulas help prepare and clean the data for analysis.

22.2 Cleaning and Preparing Data

Data cleaning and preparation is a foundational step in the data science process. This stage involves addressing missing values, detecting and managing outliers, rectifying errors in the data, and transforming variables to suitable formats. Excel boasts an extensive set of functions that assist in these tasks. Functions like IFERROR, ISBLANK, and TRIM are essential for handling errors and cleaning textual data. Similarly, Excel's Find & Replace and Conditional Formatting features streamline the data cleaning process and help prepare the data for subsequent analysis.

22.3 Exploratory Data Analysis in Excel

Exploratory Data Analysis (EDA) is a phase in the data science process that emphasizes the understanding of data characteristics. This stage often involves summarizing the data, identifying patterns, detecting anomalies, and testing hypotheses. Excel offers an arsenal of tools for EDA. PivotTables, for instance, provide an interactive way to summarize and aggregate large datasets. Excel's vast array of statistical functions facilitate in-depth data analysis, and its charting tools enable the visualization of data trends and distributions.

22.4 Building Predictive Models in Excel

Predictive modeling, a key aspect of data science, involves creating, testing, and validating a model to predict future events or outcomes. In Excel, predictive modeling can be performed using the regression analysis feature available in the Data

Analysis ToolPak or using the Solver add-in for optimization problems. Regression analysis can predict a dependent variable based on one or more independent variables, and Solver can find optimal solutions for complex problems with multiple constraints.

22.5 Visualizing Data for Data Science

Data visualization plays a vital role in data science, as it translates complex datasets into visual graphics that are easy to understand and interpret. Excel offers a comprehensive suite of data visualization tools, ranging from basic charts (like line, bar, pie, and scatter plots) to more advanced tools like conditional formatting and PivotCharts. These visualization tools make it possible to identify patterns, trends, and outliers, enabling meaningful insights to be drawn from the data.

In conclusion, Excel, with its extensive feature set, offers a robust platform for data science tasks. From the initial stages of data cleaning and preparation, through exploratory data analysis and predictive modeling, to the final stage of visualizing data, Excel equips users with the necessary tools to transform data into valuable insights.

Interactive Exercises

Exercise: Understand the data science process, clean and prepare data, perform exploratory data analysis, build predictive models, and visualize data. **Question**: How does Excel fit into the data science process, and what are the techniques for data cleaning, preparation, and visualization?

Chapter 23: Excel for Project Management

Project management encompasses the orchestration of multiple tasks, resources, and timelines to successfully achieve a specific goal. Excel's wide-ranging capabilities make it an indispensable tool for project management. This chapter delves into the ways Excel can be utilized for project management, from creating Gantt charts, tracking project tasks, managing resources, analyzing project costs, to reporting project status.

23.1 Creating Gantt Charts

Gantt charts serve as a visual tool to display project schedules, making it easy to understand task sequences, durations, and overlaps. While Excel does not offer a built-in Gantt chart, its stacked bar chart can be effectively manipulated to replicate one. This involves creating a task list on the vertical axis, with start dates, end dates, and durations, and then transforming this data into a stacked bar chart. The bars represent tasks and their durations, plotted against the timeline on the horizontal axis, providing a clear depiction of the project schedule.

23.2 Tracking Project Tasks

Efficient project management involves meticulous tracking of all project tasks. Excel provides several features that assist in this endeavor. A detailed task list can be created, complete with task descriptions, assignees, start and end dates, deadlines, priorities, status, and percent complete. Features like conditional formatting can be leveraged to visually indicate task status or impending deadlines. Additionally, Excel's filter and sort capabilities can facilitate swift navigation through tasks based on specific criteria, such as tasks assigned to a particular member or incomplete tasks.

23.3 Managing Resources

Resource management is integral to project management, ensuring efficient allocation and usage of resources. With Excel, resources such as team members, equipment, or materials can be effectively tracked and managed. You can create a resource allocation matrix that maps the quantity of each resource required for individual tasks. Excel's powerful computational functions can be used to calculate total resource usage and cost implications, and PivotTables can summarize this data, providing an overview of resource distribution and expenditure.

23.4 Analyzing Project Costs

Project costs form a critical metric in project management. Monitoring these costs helps keep the project within the budgetary constraints. Excel offers a multitude of functions for cost analysis. Formulas can calculate cumulative costs, cost averages, variances, and more. Excel's charting functionalities can aid in visualizing cost trends and disparities, aiding in budget management. Moreover, Excel's 'what-if' analysis can model how changes in costs or resource allocation would affect the overall project budget, facilitating informed decision-making.

23.5 Reporting Project Status

Keeping stakeholders updated about the project progress is crucial. Excel supports the creation of detailed project status reports. Tables and charts can visually represent data, highlighting key aspects such as task progress, resource usage, cost metrics, etc. Conditional formatting can draw attention to crucial data points, like tasks nearing deadlines or exceeding budgets. Additionally, Excel's capability to create dashboards presents a consolidated view of various data points, facilitating a quick, comprehensive understanding of the project status.

Excel, with its multifaceted features, provides a dynamic platform for project management. Whether it's planning schedules, tracking tasks, managing resources, performing cost analysis, or updating project status, Excel equips project managers with the necessary tools to steer projects towards successful completion.

Interactive Exercises

Exercise: Create Gantt charts, track project tasks, manage resources, analyze project costs, and report project status. **Question**: How can Excel support project management, and what are the tools for tracking and analyzing projects?

Chapter 24: Excel for Marketing

Marketing is a critical facet of business operations, involving a blend of research, planning, execution, and analysis to create, communicate, and deliver offerings that have value for customers. Excel, a multifunctional software, stands as a powerful ally in the execution of these marketing tasks. This chapter delves deeper into Excel's capabilities in marketing, discussing the analysis of market trends, sales forecasting, customer segment analysis, campaign performance tracking, and marketing dashboard creation.

24.1 Analyzing Market Trends

The assessment of market trends forms the bedrock of strategic decision-making in marketing. These trends reflect changes in market behavior and customer preferences over time. Excel offers an array of functionalities to perform such analysis. Line charts and bar graphs can visually represent sales or market share fluctuations over a specified period. Scatter plots can decipher correlations between different market variables, and pivot tables can summarize and distill insights from large datasets. Excel's rich library of statistical functions, such as moving averages or linear regression, can unveil underlying trends and patterns in market data.

24.2 Forecasting Sales

Sales forecasting, a pivotal component of business planning, involves predicting future sales volumes based on historical data and market trend analysis. Excel is armed with a suite of tools to aid this forecasting. The Forecast function in Excel uses historical data to predict future trends. Tools like Solver and Goal Seek can optimize sales forecasts considering certain constraints, such as budgets or resources. Additionally, Excel's Scenario Manager can perform scenario analysis, enabling marketers to gauge the impact of changes in various parameters on future sales.

24.3 Analyzing Customer Segments

Customer segmentation refers to the division of a market into distinct subsets of customers with similar needs or behaviors. Excel provides several tools for segmentation analysis. Pivot tables can group customers based on specific criteria such as demographics or purchase patterns, generating key metrics for each segment. Add-ins like Analysis ToolPak can be used to perform advanced cluster analysis, facilitating the identification of unique segments within the customer data.

24.4 Tracking Campaign Performance

Tracking the performance of marketing campaigns is crucial to gauge the effectiveness of marketing strategies and to inform future efforts. Excel allows for detailed campaign tracking. Marketers can establish a spreadsheet detailing key performance indicators (KPIs) such as impressions, clicks, conversions, and return on investment (ROI). Conditional formatting can be employed to highlight well-performing or underperforming campaigns. Excel's charting capabilities can visualize campaign performance over time, providing a clear trajectory of campaign successes or areas needing improvement.

24.5 Creating Dashboards for Marketing

Dashboards provide a comprehensive, consolidated view of various data points, offering a quick and easy understanding of marketing performance. Excel's myriad features facilitate the creation of dynamic and interactive dashboards. Pivot tables and slicers can be employed for interactive data summarization. Excel's charting capabilities can create visual representations of the data. Conditional formatting can underscore key insights or trends. Marketers can also construct dashboard reports using named ranges, data validation, and form controls, which enhance user-friendliness and the overall informative value of the dashboard.

In essence, Excel's versatility and comprehensive features make it a potent tool for marketing. Whether it's sifting through market trends, making sales forecasts, delving into customer segments, tracking campaign performance, or creating insightful dashboards, Excel enables marketers to derive profound insights from data, promoting informed and data-driven decision-making.

Interactive Exercises

Exercise: Analyze market trends, forecast sales, analyze customer segments, track campaign performance, and create marketing dashboards. **Question**: How can Excel enhance marketing analysis, and what are the methods for sales forecasting and campaign tracking?

Chapter 25: Excel for Human Resources

Human Resources (HR) is the critical function that oversees the most valuable asset of any organization—its people. Excel, with its multifaceted functionalities, is a key tool in managing HR tasks, providing efficiency and precision. This chapter delves deeper into the role of Excel in various HR scenarios, encompassing employee data tracking, turnover analysis, compensation model development, training and development analysis, and HR dashboard creation.

25.1 Tracking Employee Data

HR professionals routinely handle vast amounts of employee data, spanning demographics, employment dates, job roles, performance evaluations, and more. Excel is an invaluable tool in creating a comprehensive, dynamic employee database. Its robust data management capabilities—sorting, filtering, searching—facilitate easy navigation and analysis. Further, Excel's table feature can streamline data organization, allowing automatic expansion of data ranges and application of structured referencing.

25.2 Analyzing Employee Turnover

Employee turnover analysis is crucial in HR, helping assess employee satisfaction, retention strategies, and the organization's overall health. Excel can be used to calculate turnover rates, perform year-on-year or departmental comparisons, and discern trends. PivotTables can aggregate and dissect data, providing summarized views of turnover by department, role, or tenure. Data visualization tools, like line graphs or bar charts, can depict turnover trends and fluctuations, providing quick, intuitive insights.

25.3 Creating Compensation Models

The creation of just, motivating, and competitive compensation models is a core HR task. Excel can support this process with its vast array of financial functions. Excel allows for the calculation of various compensation elements, like base pay, bonuses, commissions, and benefits. It can model different compensation strategies, taking into account various factors such as performance ratings, market benchmarks, and internal parity. Excel's 'What-If' analysis tools, like data tables and scenario manager, can forecast the impact of potential compensation changes, aiding in strategic decision-making.

25.4 Analyzing Training and Development

Training and development are fundamental to an organization's success, improving employee skills, morale, and productivity. Excel can be used to record training program details, track completion, and assess outcomes. Using Excel's analytical capabilities, HR professionals can measure training effectiveness, correlating program participation with changes in performance metrics. Excel's charting tools can help visualize training participation and achievement, fostering informed discussions about training strategy and investment.

25.5 Creating HR Dashboards

HR dashboards consolidate key HR metrics into a single, visually appealing display, providing a snapshot of HR performance. Excel offers a suite of features for creating such dynamic, interactive dashboards. PivotTables and slicers can enable interactive data representation, charts and sparklines can visualize data trends, and conditional formatting can highlight key data points. Excel dashboards can track a myriad of HR metrics, such as headcount, turnover, recruitment status, and learning and development progress, providing a holistic overview of the organization's human capital landscape.

In summary, Excel's advanced features and capabilities make it an indispensable tool in the realm of HR. Its functionalities enhance and streamline HR tasks, from maintaining comprehensive employee databases, analyzing crucial metrics like turnover, developing and evaluating compensation strategies, assessing training initiatives, to creating informative HR dashboards. Excel, with its ease of use and versatility, thus plays a pivotal role in effective HR management.

Interactive Exercises

Exercise: Track employee data, analyze turnover, create compensation models, analyze training, and create HR dashboards. **Question**: How can Excel streamline HR processes, and what are the techniques for employee tracking and analysis?

Chapter 26: Excel for Supply Chain Management

Supply Chain Management (SCM) is a critical function that directly impacts the efficiency, cost, and profitability of an organization. SCM oversees the transformation of raw materials into final products, including all processes of procurement, inventory management, transportation, and warehousing. Microsoft Excel, with its robust features and tools, serves as a reliable companion in managing these complex processes. This chapter delves deeper into Excel's capabilities in tracking inventory, analyzing supplier performance, forecasting demand, optimizing logistics, and creating comprehensive dashboards for SCM.

26.1 Tracking Inventory

Inventory management is the backbone of any supply chain system. Excel proves an indispensable tool in creating an inventory tracking system that logs essential information about each product like SKU, product description, quantity on hand, reorder level, unit price, and lead times. Excel's built-in functions like SUM, COUNT, AVERAGE, MAX, MIN, and others are used to compute various metrics like total stock value, average selling price, and most importantly, the inventory turnover rate. Conditional formatting highlights areas that require immediate attention, such as items running low in stock or expensive items lying unsold. A well-maintained Excel inventory sheet ensures efficient inventory control, preventing stockouts and overstocks, thus optimizing inventory costs.

26.2 Analyzing Supplier Performance

A well-orchestrated supply chain relies heavily on the performance of its suppliers. Excel facilitates detailed supplier performance analysis, helping supply chain managers make data-driven decisions. Supplier data can be meticulously recorded, including delivery timelines, product quality, cost, communication efficiency, and more. Excel's PivotTables summarize this data, offering valuable insights into supplier performance. Moreover, Excel's Data Analysis ToolPak allows the execution of sophisticated statistical analyses like regression analysis and t-tests to evaluate supplier reliability and performance over time. Graphical representation of these metrics further simplifies supplier comparison and trend identification.

26.3 Forecasting Demand

Accurate demand forecasting is a cornerstone of effective SCM as it influences inventory levels, production scheduling, and logistics planning. Excel is equipped with several forecasting functions such as FORECAST.LINEAR, FORECAST.ETS, and TREND, which use historical sales data to predict future demand. Excel's Scenario Manager and Goal Seek features facilitate scenario analysis to understand the impact of different sales strategies, price points, and market conditions on demand. A robust demand forecasting model in Excel can significantly reduce the risk of overproduction or undersupply, thus optimizing resource utilization and customer satisfaction.

26.4 Optimizing Logistics

Optimization of logistics processes is pivotal in maintaining a cost-effective and efficient supply chain. Excel's powerful analytical capabilities allow detailed analysis of logistics data, including shipping times, transport costs, delivery routes, and freight capacity. These insights can help identify bottlenecks and potential areas for improvement. Excel's Solver add-in is a powerful tool for solving complex optimization problems such as determining the most economical routes, efficient loading plans, and optimal schedules to minimize cost and maximize delivery speed.

26.5 Creating Dashboards for Supply Chain Management

Dashboards are the executive summary of any data-driven process, and SCM is no exception. Excel provides a suite of tools to create dynamic, interactive dashboards that offer a comprehensive view of the supply chain metrics. PivotTables paired with slicers offer interactive data exploration, charts and sparklines visualize data patterns, and conditional formatting reveals insights otherwise hidden in heaps of data. An effective SCM dashboard tracks a wide array of metrics such as inventory turnover rate, delivery lead times, supplier performance scorecards, and demand forecast accuracy. A well-designed, informative dashboard facilitates quicker decision-making and strategy formulation.

In conclusion, Excel, with its extensive capabilities, offers numerous advantages to SCM. It supports the intricate processes of tracking inventory, analyzing supplier performance, forecasting demand, and logistics optimization, all while presenting data in a visually informative manner through dashboards. These functionalities make Excel an invaluable tool for the successful operation of SCM, leading to more profitable and efficient business outcomes.

Interactive Exercises

Exercise: Track inventory, analyze supplier performance, forecast demand, optimize logistics, and create supply chain dashboards. **Question**: How can Excel optimize supply chain operations, and what are the tools for inventory tracking and demand forecasting?

Case Study: Supply Chain Optimization for a Manufacturing Firm

- **Scenario**: A manufacturing firm uses Excel to optimize its supply chain, from tracking inventory to analyzing supplier performance.
- **Application**: Illustrate how to track inventory, forecast demand, optimize logistics, and create dashboards.
- **Outcome**: Reduced costs, improved supplier relationships, and more responsive supply chain management.

Chapter 27: Excel for Sales

Sales management is at the heart of any successful business operation, directly influencing revenue and profitability. Microsoft Excel, with its extensive suite of data management, analysis, and visualization tools, provides powerful support for this crucial function. This chapter delves into how Excel can be employed to enhance various aspects of sales management, including tracking sales data, analyzing sales trends, forecasting sales, analyzing sales performance, and creating dashboards for sales.

27.1 Tracking Sales Data

Sales data provides an overview of past transactions, offering insights into what has been sold, when, where, and to whom. Excel is well-suited for maintaining detailed sales databases, facilitating the easy recording and retrieval of information such as product SKU, quantity sold, sales price, date of sale, and customer details. With the sorting and filtering capabilities of Excel, sales teams can effectively manage this data, categorizing sales by product, region, or salesperson, and quickly retrieving information as needed. Excel's powerful PivotTable tool can then summarize this information, delivering key insights like total sales per product, average sales price, or monthly sales totals.

27.2 Analyzing Sales Trends

Understanding sales trends over time is vital for strategic decision-making. Excel provides a wide array of charting options such as line graphs, bar graphs, and scatter plots to visually represent sales trends over time. With Excel's advanced statistical functions, deeper patterns and trends in sales data can be identified. Functions like moving averages, linear regression (LINEST), or exponential smoothing (FORECAST.ETS function) can uncover underlying trends in the data, facilitating a more accurate interpretation of past sales performance and an informed prediction of future trends.

27.3 Forecasting Sales

Sales forecasting is a pivotal task in sales management, underpinning strategic planning, budgeting, and inventory management. Excel offers robust forecasting tools for this purpose. Functions like FORECAST.LINEAR or FORECAST.ETS use historical sales data to create statistically informed predictions of future sales. Moreover, Excel's what-if analysis features, including data tables and Scenario Manager, can simulate various scenarios to illustrate how changes in pricing, marketing spend, or macroeconomic factors might influence future sales.

27.4 Analyzing Sales Performance

Sales performance analysis helps assess the effectiveness of sales strategies, identify areas of strength and weakness, and guide future sales initiatives. Excel proves invaluable in this process. Key sales performance indicators such as sales volume, sales growth, sales by product/region/salesperson, and attainment of sales targets can be tracked and analyzed using Excel. Features such as conditional formatting and Sparklines can highlight areas of exceptional performance or concern. Excel's PivotCharts offer visual comparison of performance across different categories, providing a clear picture of where efforts are yielding results and where improvements are needed.

27.5 Creating Dashboards for Sales

Sales dashboards are powerful tools that consolidate key sales metrics into a single, visual display, providing a comprehensive snapshot of sales performance. Excel offers a suite of tools for creating dynamic, interactive dashboards. PivotTables and slicers can generate interactive summary tables, while various chart types can present data in a visually digestible format. Conditional formatting can draw attention to key results, and Excel's form controls like buttons, checkboxes, and sliders, can enhance dashboard interactivity and user experience.

In essence, Excel serves as a comprehensive toolkit for sales management. Its capabilities span from detailed data tracking, through insightful trend analysis and accurate sales forecasting, to thorough performance analysis and dynamic dashboard creation. By leveraging Excel's features, sales teams can extract the maximum value from their data, informing decision-making and driving sales performance.

Interactive Exercises

Exercise: Track sales data, analyze trends, forecast sales, analyze performance, and create sales dashboards. **Question**: How can Excel support sales analysis, and what are the methods for sales tracking and forecasting?

Chapter 28: Excel for Customer Service

In today's customer-centric business environment, exceptional customer service can differentiate an organization from its competitors, driving customer loyalty, positive word-of-mouth, and ultimately, business growth. Microsoft Excel, a versatile and powerful software, is instrumental in managing and optimizing customer service operations. This chapter delves into the application of Excel in customer service scenarios, including tracking customer service data, analyzing customer satisfaction, monitoring call center performance, developing service level agreements (SLAs), and creating dynamic dashboards for customer service.

28.1 Tracking Customer Service Data

A critical aspect of managing customer service is maintaining comprehensive records of customer interactions. Excel serves as a reliable platform for creating and managing databases to log various customer service parameters, including customer queries, complaints, resolution times, service agent details, and customer feedback. Excel's robust data management capabilities allow efficient sorting, filtering, and searching through this data, providing a structured and organized system for tracking customer service interactions. Functions like CONCATENATE or TEXTJOIN can create unique identifiers or standardized text entries, while date and time functions can calculate durations and track service timelines.

28.2 Analyzing Customer Satisfaction

Customer satisfaction, a critical metric reflecting the quality of an organization's customer service, can be meticulously analyzed using Excel. Customer survey results, feedback ratings, or net promoter scores can be captured in Excel, and with the use of PivotTables, the data can be summarized and analyzed across different parameters such as product, region, or service agent. Excel's statistical functions like AVERAGE, MEDIAN, MODE, or standard deviation (STDEV.S or STDEV.P) can compute satisfaction scores, and conditional formatting can highlight scores that fall below certain thresholds. This level of analysis can identify strong and weak areas in service delivery, guiding improvements.

28.3 Analyzing Call Center Performance

Call centers often form the core of a customer service operation. Excel can efficiently track and analyze critical call center metrics such as call volumes, average call duration, first call resolution rate, and customer satisfaction. Excel's data visualization capabilities, through charts and Sparklines, can represent these metrics over time, providing a clear picture of performance trends. Conditional formatting can alert supervisors to calls or agents that exceed predetermined thresholds, aiding in swift issue identification and resolution.

28.4 Creating Service Level Agreements

Service Level Agreements (SLAs) set expectations between a company and its customers regarding the standard of service to be delivered. Excel can support the creation, tracking, and management of SLAs. Functions like COUNTIF or COUNTIFS can calculate the number of instances where service levels meet, exceed, or fall short of agreed standards. Additionally, Excel's 'What-If' analysis tools, including data tables and the Scenario Manager, can simulate potential changes to service parameters, enabling proactive SLA management.

28.5 Creating Dashboards for Customer Service

Dashboards provide a snapshot of key performance indicators (KPIs), granting a quick overview of the customer service landscape. Excel, with its array of tools, enables the creation of dynamic, interactive dashboards. PivotTables, coupled with slicers, generate interactive data summaries. Various chart types present data in an easily digestible visual format. Conditional formatting can draw attention to outstanding or concerning performance. Dashboards may include a range of metrics, from customer satisfaction scores and call center performance data to SLA compliance rates and individual agent performance metrics.

In conclusion, Excel serves as a comprehensive toolkit for managing and optimizing customer service operations. Its functionalities range from detailed data tracking, through insightful trend analysis and accurate performance evaluation, to SLA management and dynamic dashboard creation. By leveraging Excel's powerful capabilities, customer service teams can make informed, data-driven decisions, driving operational excellence and delivering superior customer experiences.

Interactive Exercises

Exercise: Track customer service data, analyze satisfaction, analyze call center performance, create service level agreements, and create dashboards. **Question**: How can Excel enhance customer service analysis, and what are the techniques for satisfaction analysis and performance tracking?

Chapter 29: Excel for Operations

Operations management is a cornerstone of any business, focused on the effective design, execution, and control of operations to create maximum value. Microsoft Excel, given its robust data management, analysis, and visualization features, serves as a powerful aid for various operations management tasks, including tracking operational data, analyzing operational efficiency, creating production schedules, analyzing quality control data, and creating dashboards for operations. This chapter provides a detailed exploration of how Excel can be effectively utilized for these tasks.

29.1 Tracking Operational Data

The foundation of effective operations management is the meticulous tracking of operational data. This data spans a wide range of variables, including production volumes, production times, process times, costs, resources used, and much more. Excel provides a comprehensive platform for recording this data and maintaining a well-organized operational database. With Excel's data management capabilities, users can easily sort, filter, and search through this data, providing easy access to relevant information when needed. Conditional formatting can also be used to highlight key data points or trends in the data, facilitating quick identification of areas requiring attention.

29.2 Analyzing Operational Efficiency

Efficiency is a key metric in operations management, reflecting the optimal use of resources in the production process. Excel's vast suite of mathematical and statistical functions can be used to calculate and analyze various efficiency-related key performance indicators (KPIs), such as throughput, process cycle efficiency, capacity utilization, and overall equipment effectiveness (OEE). Furthermore, Excel's conditional formatting feature can highlight areas where efficiency is below target levels, pinpointing areas for improvement. Additionally, data visualization tools, such as Excel's array of chart options, can help visually represent efficiency trends over time, providing further insights into the operation's performance.

29.3 Creating Production Schedules

Excel is an ideal tool for creating detailed and flexible production schedules. It can be used to lay out job sequences, allocate resources, plan maintenance activities, and more. Excel's calendar and date functions can be used to create a timeline for production activities, and its Solver add-in can solve complex optimization problems, like maximizing output given resource constraints. This capability is vital in scenarios where production needs to be optimized based on various constraints, such as capacity limits, resource availability, deadlines, and priority levels.

29.4 Analyzing Quality Control Data

Quality control is an essential aspect of operations management, ensuring that products or services meet the organization's quality standards. Excel can be used to record and analyze various quality control metrics, such as defect rates, rework rates, process capability indices (Cp and Cpk), and more. With Excel's statistical functions, users can calculate key quality metrics, and Excel's charting features can be used to plot control charts, trend charts, and Pareto charts, offering visual insight into the quality of operations over time.

29.5 Creating Dashboards for Operations

Operational dashboards provide a comprehensive view of key operational metrics at a glance, enabling managers to quickly assess the performance of their operations. Excel offers a range of tools for creating dynamic, interactive dashboards that can track efficiency, productivity, quality, and other crucial operational metrics. PivotTables, slicers, and PivotCharts can be used to create interactive data summaries and visualizations. Additionally, Excel's form controls, such as buttons, checkboxes, and sliders, can enhance interactivity, allowing users to filter and explore data in real-time.

In summary, Excel provides a broad spectrum of tools and capabilities that make it a comprehensive toolkit for operations management. From tracking and analyzing operational data to creating production schedules, from ensuring quality control to developing insightful dashboards, Excel equips operations managers with the resources they need to optimize and enhance their operations. By leveraging Excel's powerful features, operations teams can ensure their processes are efficient, cost-effective, and geared for high performance.

Interactive Exercises

Exercise: Track operational data, analyze efficiency, create production schedules, analyze quality control data, and create dashboards. **Question**: How can Excel support operations management, and what are the tools for efficiency analysis and production scheduling?

Chapter 30: Excel for Accounting

Accounting forms the backbone of any business entity's financial health and operational transparency. It entails the systematic recording, sorting, and analysis of financial transactions to produce comprehensive financial reports. Microsoft Excel, with its expansive range of features, serves as an invaluable asset for accounting professionals. This chapter provides a detailed account of how Excel facilitates a myriad of accounting tasks, such as tracking financial data, crafting financial statements, analyzing financial ratios, executing variance analysis, and curating dashboards for accounting.

30.1 Tracking Financial Data

Effective accounting practices necessitate the precise and meticulous tracking of financial data. Excel excels as a tool for recording, categorizing, and organizing diverse sets of financial data, including revenue, expenses, assets, liabilities, equity, and more. Excel's robust data handling features, such as filtering, sorting, and searching, facilitate the easy retrieval and management of this data. Further, the implementation of Excel's data validation features can ensure the accuracy and consistency of the data entered, bolstering the integrity of the financial records.

30.2 Creating Financial Statements

Financial statements like the income statement, balance sheet, and cash flow statement encapsulate a business's financial performance and position. Excel's cell referencing and formula functionalities can be leveraged to construct these critical financial statements. For instance, the SUM function can aggregate revenues and expenses on the income statement, and the subtraction operator can calculate net income. Similarly, balance sheet items like total assets, total liabilities, and equity can be calculated using appropriate Excel functions, ensuring accurate, dynamic, and professional-looking financial statements.

30.3 Analyzing Financial Ratios

Financial ratios are critical for understanding the financial health and operational efficiency of a business. These include liquidity ratios (like the current and quick ratios), profitability ratios (such as gross margin and net profit margin), solvency ratios (like the debt-to-equity ratio), and efficiency ratios (like inventory turnover and accounts receivable days). Excel's arithmetic functions can be used to calculate these ratios, providing meaningful insights into the company's financial performance. Moreover, trend analysis can be performed on these ratios over time to track the company's progress and make informed financial decisions.

30.4 Performing Variance Analysis

Variance analysis is an essential component of financial management, identifying deviations between budgeted and actual figures. Excel is perfectly equipped for this task. Using Excel's various mathematical functions, the absolute and percentage variances can be calculated, providing insight into whether the actual figures are under or over the budgeted amounts. Conditional formatting can be applied to highlight significant variances, drawing immediate attention to areas that have significantly deviated from the plan and may require corrective action.

30.5 Creating Dashboards for Accounting

Accounting dashboards provide a consolidated, visual representation of key financial metrics, enabling easy monitoring and quick insights into financial performance. Excel's capabilities for creating interactive, dynamic dashboards are remarkable. Tools such as PivotTables, slicers, charts, and conditional formatting can be combined to present an overview of important financial figures like revenue, expenses, net income, cash flows, and key financial ratios. These dashboards can be designed to be user-friendly, interactive, and customizable based on the user's specific needs, providing a powerful tool for financial communication and decision-making.

In conclusion, Excel offers a comprehensive, versatile platform for performing a wide array of accounting tasks. From tracking extensive financial data and preparing dynamic financial statements to conducting deep financial analyses and presenting data through interactive dashboards, Excel empowers accounting professionals to manage and present financial information effectively and accurately. Its wide array of functionalities ensure accountants can maintain the highest standards of accuracy, efficiency, and professionalism in their work.

Interactive Exercises

Exercise: Track financial data, create financial statements, analyze ratios, perform variance analysis, and create accounting dashboards. **Question**: How can Excel streamline accounting processes, and what are the techniques for financial tracking and analysis?

Chapter 31: Excel for Auditing

Auditing serves as a critical business function, playing a pivotal role in ensuring compliance with relevant laws, regulations, and standards, enhancing operational efficiency, and improving risk management. Microsoft Excel, with its extensive suite of tools and features, stands as a veritable Swiss army knife for auditors worldwide. In this chapter, we delve deeper into Excel's capabilities for performing various audit-related tasks, such as tracking audit data, executing audit tests, analyzing audit results, generating audit reports, and crafting dashboards for auditing.

31.1 Tracking Audit Data

Auditing involves dealing with a significant amount of data, including transaction details, control information, financial data, and more. Microsoft Excel is well-equipped to handle this data, providing the capabilities to create comprehensive and organized databases. Excel's data management features such as sorting, filtering, search functions, and data validation can ensure that the audit data is accurate, reliable, and easily accessible. The integrity of audit data is critical as it forms the foundation for audit tests and subsequent conclusions.

31.2 Performing Audit Tests

Audit tests or audit procedures are conducted to gather sufficient, appropriate audit evidence. Excel provides a multitude of functions to perform these tests. For instance, Excel's mathematical and logical functions can be used to conduct analytical procedures, verifying the accuracy of recorded amounts. Excel's conditional formatting can highlight transactions or balances that fail certain tests or exceed specified thresholds. The powerful 'What-If Analysis' tools can also be employed to perform sensitivity analysis on the financial data, assessing the impact of changes in key assumptions.

31.3 Analyzing Audit Results

Once the audit tests are completed, the resulting data needs to be analyzed to draw meaningful conclusions. Excel's powerful calculation and data visualization features come in handy for this purpose. PivotTables can be used to summarize and analyze large amounts of data, providing insights into patterns and trends. Excel's array of chart options can provide visual representations of the audit results, making the findings more intuitive and easier to comprehend. Statistical functions can also be employed to identify significant deviations or anomalies in the data.

31.4 Creating Audit Reports

The final step in the audit process is reporting the audit findings. An audit report typically includes a summary of the procedures performed, findings, and the auditor's opinion. Excel offers a host of features to generate these reports in a professional and organized manner. The use of Excel tables, cell styles, and formatting tools can enhance the readability and presentation of the report. Additionally, Excel's printing features can help in ensuring that the report prints correctly, maintaining its professional appearance.

31.5 Creating Dashboards for Auditing

Dashboards serve as a powerful tool for presenting a snapshot of the audit's key findings. Excel provides a range of tools and features to create interactive, dynamic dashboards that can effectively communicate the audit results. Features such as PivotTables and PivotCharts can be used to summarize and visualize key audit metrics. Interactive elements like slicers and form controls can be added to the dashboard to allow users to filter and analyze the data in different ways. Excel's conditional formatting can highlight areas of concern or interest, drawing attention to the most significant audit findings.

In conclusion, Excel serves as a comprehensive toolkit for auditing tasks. It provides a vast array of features to streamline data tracking, facilitate audit tests, enable in-depth analysis of audit results, create professional audit reports, and build interactive dashboards. By mastering these Excel capabilities, auditors can improve their efficiency and effectiveness, providing greater value to their organizations and clients.

Interactive Exercises

Exercise: Track audit data, perform audit tests, analyze results, create reports, and create dashboards. **Question:** How can Excel support auditing processes, and what are the methods for audit tracking and analysis?

Chapter 32: Excel for Risk Management

Risk management, the process of identifying, analyzing, and responding to risk factors throughout the life of a project, plays a crucial role in the success of organizations. Effective risk management can lead to significant business and operational benefits. In this endeavor, Microsoft Excel emerges as a versatile tool, assisting risk management professionals in their vital tasks. This chapter provides an in-depth examination of how Excel can support various risk management activities, including tracking risk data, performing risk factor analyses, establishing risk models, conducting risk assessments, and curating dashboards for risk management.

32.1 Tracking Risk Data

Accurate tracking and management of risk data form the backbone of any successful risk management strategy. Excel allows the creation and maintenance of a risk register – a comprehensive document that details all potential risks, their probability of occurrence, potential impact, mitigation plans, and responsible personnel. Using Excel's extensive data validation tools, one can ensure the integrity of the data entered, thus maintaining the reliability of the risk register. Excel's powerful data handling capabilities like filtering, sorting, and search functions simplify the task of managing this vast array of risk data, leading to more efficient risk management.

32.2 Analyzing Risk Factors

With a detailed risk register at hand, the next pivotal step is the analysis of these risk factors. Excel offers a suite of advanced analytical tools for this purpose. You can use Excel's suite of statistical functions to quantify the potential impact and likelihood of risks. For example, the CORREL function can be used to understand the correlation between different risk factors, helping to identify if multiple risks are likely to occur together. Analyzing risk factors allows organizations to understand better the risks they face and make informed decisions about mitigating them.

32.3 Creating Risk Models

Risk models are integral to risk management as they allow the simulation of various scenarios, helping understand the potential impact of different risks. Excel's Scenario Manager and Data Tables, part of its What-If Analysis tools, can be used to create these models. For more complex simulations like Monte Carlo analysis, which involves running many scenarios with different random inputs, there are multiple Excel add-ins available. These tools allow risk managers to anticipate the effects of various risk scenarios and plan accordingly.

32.4 Performing Risk Assessments

Risk assessment involves determining the magnitude of potential risks by evaluating the likelihood and potential impact of identified risks. Excel, with its vast array of mathematical functions, can support this process. For instance, risks can be rated on their likelihood and impact on a scale of 1-5, and a risk score can be calculated using simple multiplication. This allows for easy comparison of risks and helps prioritize them. Furthermore, Excel's conditional formatting feature can be used to create a risk heat map, providing a visual representation of the risk landscape.

32.5 Creating Dashboards for Risk Management

Dashboards are powerful tools for summarizing and presenting risk information. Excel's features like PivotTables, PivotCharts, and slicers can be used to create dynamic, interactive dashboards that offer a high-level view of the organization's risk profile. By presenting key risk indicators visually, dashboards can make it easier for decision-makers to understand the organization's exposure to risk and monitor changes over time. This, in turn, facilitates informed decision-making and helps ensure effective risk management.

In conclusion, Excel is an indispensable tool in the risk management process, providing powerful features that can be used to track risk data, analyze risk factors, model risk scenarios, assess risk, and present risk information. Excel's capabilities in handling large volumes of data, performing complex calculations, and creating professional-looking reports and dashboards make it a popular choice among risk management professionals. By mastering the Excel features discussed in this chapter, one can enhance their risk management efforts, leading to improved project outcomes and organizational success.

Interactive Exercises

Exercise: Track risk data, analyze risk factors, create risk models, perform assessments, and create dashboards. **Question**: How can Excel facilitate risk management, and what are the tools for risk tracking and assessment?

Chapter 33: Excel for Quality Management

Quality management, encompassing all activities and tasks needed to maintain a desired level of excellence, is an indispensable aspect of every organization. Excel, a powerful spreadsheet program, brings forth an extensive suite of features, making it an ideal tool for supporting various aspects of quality management. This chapter offers a detailed exploration of how Excel facilitates different quality management activities, such as tracking quality data, performing in-depth analysis of quality metrics, constructing quality control charts, conducting root cause analysis, and developing dashboards for quality management.

33.1 Tracking Quality Data

At the heart of quality management lies accurate and comprehensive tracking of quality data. This data includes a broad spectrum of metrics, from process measurements and inspection data to deviations and defects. Excel provides robust data management functionalities to create, manage, and update such quality data databases. It offers tools for data validation to ensure that the data input meets certain conditions, thus preventing the entry of incorrect data. Excel's data sorting and filtering capabilities, combined with its powerful search function, also make it straightforward to navigate through large volumes of data, simplifying data retrieval and modification.

33.2 Analyzing Quality Metrics

Once the quality data has been accurately captured and organized, it's time for analysis. This step allows organizations to gain insights from their data, guiding them to take necessary actions to improve their quality standards. Excel's wide range of statistical functions can be utilized to perform these analytical tasks. For instance, measures of central tendency (like mean, median) and measures of dispersion (like variance, standard deviation) can be easily calculated using built-in Excel functions. Moreover, Excel's conditional formatting feature can highlight data points that meet certain conditions, thus drawing attention to significant anomalies or trends.

33.3 Creating Quality Control Charts

Quality control charts are widely used in quality management to monitor process variability over time. Excel, with its versatile charting capabilities, is a perfect tool to construct various types of control charts like X-bar and R charts, p-charts, and c-charts. Such charts, while tracking quality metrics, can also assist in identifying if a process is in a state of statistical control or if there are out-of-control conditions indicating a need for corrective actions.

33.4 Performing Root Cause Analysis

Root cause analysis is a critical aspect of quality management. It aims to identify the underlying cause of a problem or defect, thereby preventing its recurrence. Excel can support this analysis in several ways. A fishbone diagram, a popular visual tool for categorizing potential causes of a problem, can be created using Excel's drawing tools. In addition to this, one can use Excel's data analysis capabilities to sift through the data and pinpoint the significant factors contributing to the issue.

33.5 Creating Dashboards for Quality Management

Dashboards play a pivotal role in presenting a holistic view of the organization's quality performance. They serve as visual tools for communicating key quality metrics to stakeholders. Excel's data visualization tools, such as PivotTables, PivotCharts, slicers, and conditional formatting, make the process of creating interactive, informative dashboards straightforward. These dashboards can reflect a variety of quality data, from defect rates to process capability indices, giving stakeholders a quick snapshot of the organization's quality performance and enabling prompt decision-making.

In summary, Excel is a comprehensive tool that can significantly streamline and enhance various quality management activities. From maintaining extensive databases of quality data, through facilitating insightful analysis of quality metrics, to developing visually impactful dashboards, Excel equips quality management professionals with the tools they need to ensure the delivery of high-quality products or services. Its capabilities contribute significantly to an organization's pursuit of quality excellence.

Interactive Exercises

Exercise: Track quality data, analyze metrics, create control charts, perform root cause analysis, and create dashboards. **Question**: How can Excel enhance quality management, and what are the techniques for quality tracking and analysis?

Case Study: Quality Control in a Food Processing Plant

- **Scenario**: A food processing plant uses Excel for quality control, tracking quality data, and analyzing metrics.
- **Application**: Explain how to create quality control charts, perform root cause analysis, and create dashboards.
- **Outcome**: Enhanced product quality, compliance with regulations, and increased customer satisfaction.

Chapter 34: Excel for Healthcare

The healthcare industry is a data-intensive sector, generating, and using a wide range of data to drive care delivery. Harnessing the power of this data is crucial for effective healthcare management, including patient care, outcome analysis, treatment planning, cost management, and more. Microsoft Excel, known for its advanced data management and analysis capabilities, can be a potent tool in the hands of healthcare professionals. This chapter offers a more comprehensive look into how Excel can be used for various healthcare-related tasks such as tracking patient data, analyzing health outcomes, formulating treatment plans, scrutinizing healthcare costs, and designing dashboards for healthcare.

34.1 Tracking Patient Data

Patient data forms the core of any healthcare system. It encompasses a variety of information, from demographic details and medical histories to diagnostic results and medication records. Excel provides a well-structured, flexible environment for storing and managing this vast array of data. Using Excel's data validation tools, healthcare professionals can ensure the entry of consistent and correct data, minimizing the risk of inaccuracies that could impact patient care. Moreover, Excel's powerful data management functions, including sorting, filtering, and searching, simplify the task of navigating and organizing patient data, allowing for quick and easy access to pertinent patient information. Excel's features like password protection and data encryption can also help maintain data security, which is crucial given the sensitive nature of patient data.

34.2 Analyzing Health Outcomes

A critical aspect of healthcare is the ability to analyze health outcomes effectively and efficiently. These outcomes can be influenced by a wide array of factors, and a thorough analysis is key to understanding and improving them. Excel comes equipped with a broad range of statistical functions and graphing tools that can be employed for this purpose. For instance, PivotTables can be used to generate summary statistics, identify trends, and make comparisons, while Excel's charting capabilities can provide visual representations of these data, facilitating intuitive and insightful interpretations. Excel can be utilized to calculate and analyze key metrics such as mortality rates, readmission rates, patient satisfaction scores, average length of hospital stay, and many others.

34.3 Creating Treatment Plans

The creation of structured, personalized treatment plans is a significant part of healthcare delivery. These plans can include information about prescribed medications, therapy schedules, lifestyle recommendations, and more. Excel can be leveraged to create and manage these treatment plans in a systematic manner. For instance, Excel's date and time functions can be used to create treatment schedules, while its ability to link data across worksheets can help keep patient data, medication information, and treatment plans interconnected. Excel's flexibility allows these plans to be readily updated and modified as the patient's treatment progresses, ensuring the delivery of timely and appropriate care.

34.4 Analyzing Healthcare Costs

Healthcare costs represent a critical aspect of healthcare management. The escalating costs of healthcare services globally necessitate careful tracking and analysis. Excel can serve as a potent tool for tracking and scrutinizing these costs. It can be used to perform cost comparisons, budget analyses, and financial forecasting. For instance, Excel's financial functions can be used to analyze and compare the costs of different treatment options. Conditional formatting can be applied to highlight areas of concern, such as cost overruns, aiding in prompt identification and rectification of such issues.

34.5 Creating Dashboards for Healthcare

In the data-dense healthcare environment, dashboards serve as a valuable tool for condensing and presenting key information in an easy-to-understand, visual format. Dashboards can track and display key healthcare metrics, patient outcomes, costs, and more. Excel's data visualization tools, such as charts, PivotTables, slicers, and form controls, make the creation of dynamic, interactive dashboards a straightforward process. For instance, a healthcare dashboard in Excel might include a mix of tables and charts showing patient demographic data, key health metrics, trends in patient outcomes, and financial data, allowing for an at-a-glance view of critical information.

In conclusion, Microsoft Excel provides a comprehensive toolkit for managing and analyzing healthcare data. From maintaining extensive patient databases, conducting robust health outcome analyses, formulating dynamic treatment plans, to performing meticulous healthcare cost analysis and creating visually appealing dashboards, Excel equips healthcare professionals with the resources they need to deliver more informed, efficient, and effective patient care. By leveraging Excel's capabilities, healthcare professionals can not only enhance their everyday operations but also contribute to better health outcomes and improved patient experiences.

Interactive Exercises

Exercise: Track patient data, analyze health outcomes, create treatment plans, analyze costs, and create dashboards. **Question**: How can Excel support healthcare management, and what are the methods for patient tracking and cost analysis?

Chapter 35: Excel for Education

Education is a sector where data drives a multitude of decisions, from individual student progress tracking to institutional performance evaluations. Microsoft Excel, with its robust features for data management, analysis, and visualization, can be an invaluable tool in the realm of education. This chapter provides an in-depth exploration of how Excel can be utilized to track student data, analyze test scores, devise lesson plans, evaluate school performance, and create insightful dashboards for education.

35.1 Tracking Student Data

In the field of education, student data forms the foundation of many crucial processes like performance evaluation, personalized learning plan development, and student behavior management. This data spans various dimensions including demographic details, academic performance data, attendance records, and more. Excel presents a well-structured, intuitive platform for storing, managing, and manipulating this critical data. With Excel's data validation tools, educators can ensure the accuracy and consistency of the data entered, thus reducing the risk of errors. Furthermore, Excel's data sorting and filtering features, along with its efficient search function, make it easy to organize, navigate, and retrieve specific student data. The ability to password-protect Excel worksheets adds an extra layer of security to sensitive student data.

35.2 Analyzing Test Scores

Test scores represent a critical measure of student learning and understanding, and their analysis is key to gauging student progress and identifying areas for improvement. Excel offers a wide range of statistical functions and analysis tools that can simplify and enhance this process. Educators can leverage Excel to calculate various statistical measures such as mean scores, score distributions, percentiles, and standard deviations. More advanced analytical functions like correlation and regression can be used to identify relationships between different factors affecting test scores. Excel's charting capabilities further allow educators to visualize these analytical results, making patterns and trends easier to understand.

35.3 Creating Lesson Plans

Lesson planning is a fundamental task in education, requiring both organization and flexibility. Excel serves as an excellent tool for creating, managing, and modifying lesson plans. With Excel's grid layout and cell formatting features, educators can outline lessons by various timeframes (daily, weekly, monthly), incorporate essential details such as learning objectives, instructional strategies, assessment methods, and required resources, and adjust these plans as the course progresses. The use of hyperlinks within Excel can also provide quick access to digital resources, making lesson plans even more dynamic and interactive.

35.4 Analyzing School Performance

Assessing school or institutional performance is a critical part of educational management. Excel's advanced data analysis capabilities can be employed to evaluate a range of performance indicators, such as overall test scores, attendance rates, graduation rates, and more. Excel's PivotTable feature is particularly beneficial for these tasks. PivotTables can compile, summarize, and present data in a user-friendly format, enabling comparisons between different classes, grades, or schools and identifying trends and patterns over time.

35.5 Creating Dashboards for Education

Data visualization is a potent tool in education, facilitating the understanding of complex educational data. Excel can be used to create interactive and dynamic dashboards, providing a summary view of key educational metrics. A well-crafted dashboard might display a range of information, from individual student progress and class performance to broader institutional data. Excel's data visualization tools, including charts, PivotTables, slicers, and conditional formatting, make the creation of these dashboards a relatively straightforward process.

To conclude, Excel, with its comprehensive suite of features, serves as a powerful tool in the realm of education. Whether it's tracking and managing student data, conducting sophisticated test score analyses, formulating flexible lesson plans, assessing school performance, or creating insightful educational dashboards, Excel supports educators in myriad ways. By harnessing Excel's capabilities, educators can facilitate data-driven decision-making, enhance educational processes, and contribute to improved learning outcomes.

Interactive Exercises

Exercise: Track student data, analyze test scores, create lesson plans, analyze school performance, and create dashboards. **Question**: How can Excel enhance educational processes, and what are the tools for student tracking and performance analysis?

Chapter 36: Excel for Real Estate

The real estate industry revolves around vast amounts of data related to properties, markets, transactions, and more. Understanding and leveraging this data can be the difference between successful and unsuccessful real estate operations. Microsoft Excel, with its extensive capabilities for data handling, analysis, and visualization, can be an invaluable tool for real estate professionals. This chapter delves deeper into how Excel can be employed for tracking property data, analyzing market trends, building financial models for real estate, scrutinizing property investments, and creating insightful dashboards for real estate.

36.1 Tracking Property Data

Effective property data management is at the core of real estate operations. This involves maintaining diverse property-related data, including property specifications, geographic location, list and sale prices, rental income (for investment properties), property status (e.g., available, under contract, sold), and more. Excel provides an intuitive and flexible platform for recording, organizing, and accessing this critical data. Its powerful data management features, such as sorting and filtering, facilitate efficient data navigation and retrieval. Additionally, Excel's capabilities for creating custom data categories and labels add another layer of flexibility, allowing real estate professionals to tailor their data management system to their specific needs.

36.2 Analyzing Market Trends

In the ever-changing real estate industry, staying abreast of market trends is crucial. Market trends can include changes in property prices, rental yields, buyer preferences, neighborhood developments, and more. Excel's wide range of data analysis and visualization tools can be employed to scrutinize these trends and draw actionable insights. PivotTables can summarize and pivot large datasets to highlight key trends, while Excel's diverse charting capabilities can visually represent these trends, making them easier to understand and communicate. Using Excel's statistical functions, professionals can calculate trend-related metrics and perform more sophisticated market analyses.

36.3 Creating Financial Models for Real Estate

Real estate operations, particularly those related to property investment, require detailed financial analyses. These can involve scenarios such as calculating potential return on an investment property, analyzing cash flows, determining property valuation, or projecting the impact of a mortgage on cash flow. Excel, with its comprehensive array of financial functions, is an excellent tool for creating these financial models. Real estate professionals can use functions like PMT for mortgage payment calculations, NPV for net present value analysis, IRR for internal rate of return calculations, and many more. Excel's flexibility enables these models to be readily adjusted based on different assumptions or changing market conditions.

36.4 Analyzing Property Investments

Property investment is a significant aspect of real estate, involving detailed financial and market analyses to assess potential returns and associated risks. Excel's financial and statistical functions can be employed to compute key investment metrics such as cash-on-cash return, capitalization rate, return on investment, and others. Real estate professionals can use Excel to conduct comparative analyses of different investment opportunities, analyze investment risks, and ultimately make informed investment decisions.

36.5 Creating Dashboards for Real Estate

In the data-intensive real estate environment, dashboards serve as an essential tool for summarizing and presenting key information in an easily digestible format. Excel offers a suite of data visualization tools that can be used to create comprehensive real estate dashboards. A well-designed dashboard can provide an at-a-glance view of various key indicators such as property data, market trends, portfolio performance, and investment returns. Excel's features like charts, PivotTables, conditional formatting, and form controls enable the creation of dynamic, interactive dashboards that can significantly enhance data analysis and decision-making processes.

In conclusion, Excel provides an extensive suite of tools that can significantly enhance various aspects of real estate management. From efficient property data management and insightful market trend analyses to comprehensive financial modeling and user-friendly dashboard creation, Excel supports real estate professionals in making informed, data-driven decisions. By effectively harnessing Excel's capabilities, real estate professionals can enhance their operational efficiency, make informed decisions, and ultimately drive successful real estate operations.

Interactive Exercises

Exercise: Track property data, analyze market trends, create financial models, analyze investments, and create dashboards. **Question**: How can Excel support real estate analysis, and what are the methods for property tracking and investment analysis?

Chapter 37: Excel for Nonprofits

Nonprofit organizations, while working towards societal and environmental causes, handle a vast array of data. From donor records and fundraising statistics to budget allocations and program outcomes, each facet of a nonprofit's operation involves data. Efficient data management and insightful data analysis can significantly enhance a nonprofit's operations, decision-making, and impact. Microsoft Excel, with its wide-ranging data management, analysis, and visualization features, can be a critical tool in the arsenal of nonprofits. This chapter offers an in-depth look at how Excel can be utilized for tracking donor data, analyzing fundraising campaigns, creating budgets, examining program outcomes, and generating insightful dashboards for nonprofits.

37.1 Tracking Donor Data

At the heart of many nonprofit organizations are their donors, whose contributions enable the organization to achieve its mission. Effective donor data management is thus crucial, involving the tracking of diverse information like donor contact details, donation amounts and dates, payment methods, donor engagement levels, and more. Excel provides a systematic and organized platform for recording and handling this critical data. With Excel's data validation tools, data entry errors can be minimized, ensuring accuracy and consistency. Furthermore, Excel's data filtering and sorting functionalities simplify the task of navigating large datasets, enabling quick retrieval of specific donor information when needed.

37.2 Analyzing Fundraising Campaigns

Fundraising campaigns form the lifeline of many nonprofits, generating the funds necessary for their operations and initiatives. Therefore, assessing the success of these campaigns is essential. Excel offers powerful data analysis tools that can provide deep insights into fundraising campaign performance. Excel can help track various campaign metrics, such as funds raised, donor participation, cost per dollar raised, and more. With PivotTables, campaign data can be summarized and pivoted to reveal key patterns and trends. Additionally, Excel's conditional formatting can highlight campaigns that met or exceeded their goals, providing visual cues to identify successful fundraising initiatives.

37.3 Creating Budgets for Nonprofits

Budgets are the financial blueprints that guide a nonprofit's operations, making budget management a key aspect of a nonprofit's financial health. Excel can be a pivotal tool in creating detailed, flexible budgets that track income and expenditure. With Excel, nonprofits can allocate resources efficiently, keep track of spending against the budget, and ensure financial sustainability. Excel's wide range of formulas and functions automate budget calculations, saving time and reducing errors. Additionally, Excel's charting capabilities can visualize budget data, simplifying the task of understanding and presenting budget information to stakeholders.

37.4 Analyzing Program Outcomes

Nonprofits conduct various programs aimed at fulfilling their mission. Analyzing the outcomes of these programs is essential to gauge their effectiveness, identify success areas, and pinpoint areas for improvement. Excel can assist in tracking program data and measuring outcomes against predefined objectives. Excel's array of statistical functions can be leveraged to conduct these analyses, providing valuable insights that can inform future program development and execution.

37.5 Creating Dashboards for Nonprofits

In the data-driven world of nonprofits, dashboards serve as a vital tool for summarizing and presenting key data in an easily digestible format. Excel offers a suite of data visualization tools that can be used to create dynamic, interactive dashboards. These dashboards can display an array of key metrics like donations received, fundraising campaign performance, budget utilization, and program outcomes. Excel's data visualization elements like charts, PivotTables, and slicers, in conjunction with interactive controls like form controls and timelines, can be used to create comprehensive dashboards that provide a snapshot of the nonprofit's operations.

In conclusion, Excel provides an extensive toolkit that can significantly enhance various aspects of nonprofit management. From meticulous donor data management and insightful fundraising campaign analyses to comprehensive budget creation and program outcome evaluation, Excel supports nonprofits in making informed, data-driven decisions. By effectively leveraging Excel's capabilities, nonprofits can enhance their operational efficiency, effectiveness, and ultimately, the impact of their work.

Interactive Exercises

Exercise: Track donor data, analyze fundraising campaigns, create budgets, analyze program outcomes, and create dashboards. **Question**: How can Excel enhance nonprofit management, and what are the techniques for donor tracking and fundraising analysis?

Case Study: Fundraising Analysis for a Nonprofit Organization

- **Scenario**: A nonprofit organization uses Excel to analyze fundraising campaigns, track donor data, and create budgets.
- **Application**: Demonstrate how to track donor data, analyze fundraising campaigns, and create dashboards.
- **Outcome**: Increased fundraising efficiency, more effective donor engagement, and better alignment with organizational goals.

Chapter 38: Excel for Personal Finance

Personal finance is a critical aspect of every individual's life, encompassing the management of income, expenses, savings, investments, and retirement planning. Excel, with its extensive range of features and functionalities, can be a powerful tool for effective personal finance management. In this chapter, we will delve deep into how Excel can be utilized to its fullest potential for tracking personal finances, creating comprehensive budgets, conducting investment analysis, planning for retirement, and developing insightful dashboards that offer a clear overview of one's financial health.

38.1 Tracking Personal Finances

A solid understanding of one's financial situation begins with meticulous tracking of income and expenses. Excel provides an organized platform for recording financial transactions, categorizing income sources, monitoring regular expenses, and tracking irregular or unexpected costs. Users can set up worksheets to capture details such as date, description, amount, and category for each transaction. Excel's powerful sorting, filtering, and grouping functionalities enable efficient data management, making it easy to retrieve specific financial information whenever required.

38.2 Creating Personal Budgets

Budgeting is an indispensable practice for managing personal finances effectively. With Excel's extensive calculation capabilities, users can create dynamic and comprehensive budgets that accommodate income streams, fixed expenses, variable expenses, savings goals, debt repayments, and more. Excel's conditional formatting can be utilized to visually identify budget variances, ensuring adherence to financial goals. Additionally, the use of Excel's data validation tools can prevent the entry of erroneous data, enhancing the accuracy of budgeting.

38.3 Analyzing Investments

Investment analysis is crucial for individuals seeking to build and grow their wealth. Excel offers an array of financial functions that enable users to assess investment options with precision. By calculating metrics such as compound interest, future value, present value, and return on investment, users can evaluate potential returns and risks associated with different investment vehicles. Excel's scenario analysis allows individuals to simulate various investment scenarios based on different assumptions, empowering them to make informed investment decisions aligned with their financial objectives and risk tolerance.

38.4 Planning for Retirement

Planning for retirement is a long-term financial goal that requires careful consideration and foresight. Excel can play a vital role in developing comprehensive retirement plans that encompass factors such as current savings, future contributions, anticipated expenses, inflation rates, and expected retirement age. Excel's advanced modeling capabilities enable users to simulate different retirement scenarios, assessing the impact of varying variables on their retirement funds. By examining these scenarios, individuals can make strategic decisions to achieve their retirement goals.

38.5 Creating Dashboards for Personal Finance

Effective visualization of financial data is key to gaining valuable insights into one's financial health. Excel's data visualization tools, including various chart types, PivotTables, and slicers, empower users to create dynamic and interactive dashboards. These dashboards can present key financial metrics, visualize trends, and facilitate data-driven decision-making. Users can customize their dashboards to showcase personalized financial goals and track progress towards achieving them. By regularly updating the dashboard, individuals can monitor their financial trajectory and make adjustments to improve their financial position.

In conclusion, Excel's versatile capabilities make it an indispensable tool for personal finance management. By harnessing Excel's potential for tracking finances, creating budgets, analyzing investments, planning for retirement, and developing insightful dashboards, individuals can gain a comprehensive view of their financial situation. Through proactive financial management with Excel, individuals can make informed decisions, maintain financial stability, and work towards achieving their short-term and long-term financial aspirations.

Interactive Exercises

Exercise: Track personal finances, create budgets, analyze investments, plan for retirement, and create dashboards. **Question**: How can Excel support personal finance management, and what are the tools for budgeting and investment analysis?

Chapter 39: Excel Tips and Tricks

Excel is a versatile and powerful spreadsheet software that is widely used across various industries and professions. While many users are familiar with basic Excel functions, there are numerous tips and tricks that can significantly enhance productivity, streamline workflows, and unlock the full potential of the software. In this chapter, we will delve deep into a range of valuable Excel tips and tricks, covering keyboard shortcuts, customizing the Excel interface, troubleshooting common issues, implementing best practices for efficient usage, and staying updated with the latest features in Excel 2023.

39.1 Using Keyboard Shortcuts

Keyboard shortcuts are an essential component of Excel mastery, enabling users to perform tasks quickly and efficiently. Excel offers an extensive array of keyboard shortcuts for common operations such as navigation, selection, formatting, and formula entry. Learning and incorporating these shortcuts into daily Excel usage can save significant time and reduce reliance on mouse-clicks. Moreover, users can customize keyboard shortcuts to suit their preferences and work style, further enhancing their efficiency.

39.2 Customizing the Excel Interface

Excel's flexibility allows users to customize the interface to align with their specific needs and optimize their workflow. The Quick Access Toolbar can be personalized to include frequently used commands, such as "Save," "Print," or custom macros. Users can also create custom Ribbon tabs to group related commands or create custom Excel templates that contain specific formatting and calculations. By organizing the interface to prioritize essential functions, users can reduce the clutter and streamline their Excel experience.

39.3 Troubleshooting Common Issues

While Excel is a powerful tool, users may encounter occasional challenges or errors while working with complex data or formulas. Excel provides several tools and features to assist in troubleshooting. The "Error Checking" function can identify and help resolve formula errors, and the "Evaluate Formula" tool allows users to step through complex calculations to pinpoint issues. Understanding these troubleshooting techniques empowers users to identify and rectify errors swiftly, ensuring data accuracy and reliability.

39.4 Excel Best Practices

Adhering to best practices is crucial for creating efficient and error-free Excel workbooks. Consistent data organization, using meaningful labels and clear headings, avoiding merged cells, and utilizing named ranges are among the fundamental best practices for data management. Additionally, implementing data validation rules and conditional formatting can enhance data quality and visual clarity. Embracing these best practices fosters consistency, simplifies data analysis, and facilitates collaboration with others.

39.5 Staying Updated with Excel 2023

Excel continues to evolve with each new version, introducing innovative features and improvements to enhance user experience. Staying updated with Excel 2023 ensures that users have access to the latest tools and functionalities. Microsoft's official website, Excel blogs, online tutorials, and community forums are excellent resources for learning about new features, tips, and tricks. Regularly exploring these resources empowers users to adapt quickly to changes and harness the full potential of Excel.

In conclusion, mastering Excel tips and tricks empowers users to become proficient and efficient in their spreadsheet tasks. By embracing keyboard shortcuts, customizing the interface, troubleshooting effectively, implementing best practices, and staying abreast of Excel 2023 updates, users can optimize their Excel experience and excel in data analysis, reporting, and decision-making tasks. Excel's immense capabilities combined with a comprehensive understanding of these tips and tricks elevate users to become Excel power users in their professional endeavors.

Chapter 40: Conclusion

40.1 Review of Key Concepts

Throughout this extensive book on Excel, we have delved deep into a wide array of key concepts, features, and functionalities that Excel offers to users. From the basics of navigating the Excel interface to the intricacies of advanced data analysis, we have covered fundamental skills and explored advanced techniques that empower individuals to leverage Excel's full potential for a myriad of tasks, ranging from personal finance management to complex data modeling and business analytics.

We began by understanding the Excel interface, including the Ribbon, Quick Access Toolbar, and various views for optimal data visualization and manipulation. Exploring the core functionalities of Excel, we learned how to input and edit data, use AutoFill for rapid data entry, and insert or delete cells, rows, and columns to organize information effectively.

40.2 Resources for Further Learning

Excel is a versatile tool, and there is always more to learn. For those seeking to deepen their Excel expertise, numerous resources are available. Online courses, e-books, blogs, and community forums offer valuable insights, tips, and tricks from Excel enthusiasts and experts. Microsoft's official documentation and support pages provide comprehensive guidance on various Excel features and capabilities.

40.3 Excel Certification Options

For professionals aiming to validate their Excel skills and enhance their career prospects, Microsoft offers a range of Excel certifications. These certifications, such as Microsoft Office Specialist (MOS) or Microsoft Certified: Data Analyst Associate, are recognized globally and demonstrate an individual's competence in using Excel for various tasks, making them valuable credentials for career advancement.

40.4 The Future of Excel

As technology continues to advance, so will Excel. With each new version, Microsoft introduces innovative features and enhancements, expanding Excel's capabilities and improving user experience. The future of Excel promises exciting opportunities, including more sophisticated data analysis tools, enhanced visualization options, seamless integration with cloud-based services, and improved collaboration features.

40.5 Final Thoughts

Excel has remained an essential tool for data management, analysis, and reporting for decades. Its adaptability and extensive range of features have made it a go-to solution for professionals across diverse industries. As you conclude this book, remember that mastering Excel is an ongoing journey. Embrace continuous learning, explore new features and functionalities, and challenge yourself with complex projects to sharpen your Excel skills.

Excel's power lies not only in its technical capabilities but also in its ability to turn data into actionable insights. Whether you are managing finances, analyzing business data, or conducting research, Excel empowers you to make informed decisions and solve problems creatively.

As you navigate your personal and professional endeavors, may your Excel proficiency be a valuable asset in achieving your goals. Harness the full potential of Excel, and let it be the tool that propels you towards success. Happy Excel-ing!

Excel 2023 Shortcut Cheat Sheet

Keyboard shortcuts can significantly speed up your workflow in Excel. Here are some shortcuts used in Excel 2023 :

1. Navigation Shortcuts:

- Move One Cell Up: ↑
- Move One Cell Down: ↓
- Move One Cell Left: ←
- Move One Cell Right: →
- Move to Beginning of Row: Home
- Move to Beginning of Worksheet: Ctrl + Home
- Move to End of Row: End + →
- Move to End of Worksheet: Ctrl + End

2. Selection Shortcuts:

- Select Entire Row: Shift + Space
- Select Entire Column: Ctrl + Space
- Select All Cells: Ctrl + A

3. Editing Shortcuts:

- Cut: Ctrl + X
- Copy: Ctrl + C
- Paste: Ctrl + V
- Undo: Ctrl + Z
- Redo: Ctrl + Y
- Find: Ctrl + F
- Replace: Ctrl + H

4. Formatting Shortcuts:

- Bold: Ctrl + B
- Italics: Ctrl + I
- Underline: Ctrl + U
- Strikethrough: Ctrl + 5
- Increase Font Size: Alt + H + FG
- Decrease Font Size: Alt + H + FK
- Apply Number Format: Ctrl + Shift + 1
- Apply Date Format: Ctrl + Shift + 3

5. Formula Shortcuts:

- Insert Function: Shift + F3
- Start a New Formula: =
- Toggle Absolute and Relative References: F4
- AutoSum: Alt + =

6. Workbook and Worksheet Shortcuts:

- New Workbook: Ctrl + N
- Open Workbook: Ctrl + O
- Save Workbook: Ctrl + S

- Close Workbook: Ctrl + W
- Insert New Worksheet: Shift + F11
- Move Between Worksheets: Ctrl + Page Up/Page Down

7. Data Management Shortcuts:

- Sort Ascending: Alt + H + S + A
- Sort Descending: Alt + H + S + D
- Filter: Ctrl + Shift + L
- Refresh All Connections: Ctrl + Alt + F5

8. View Shortcuts:

- Zoom In: Alt + W + Q + Q
- Zoom Out: Alt + W + Q + W
- Freeze Panes: Alt + W + F + F
- Split Window: Alt + W + S

9. PivotTable Shortcuts:

- Create a PivotTable: Alt + N + V
- Refresh PivotTable: Alt + F5

10. Chart Shortcuts:

- Create Chart: Alt + F1
- Create Chart in a New Worksheet: F11

11. Accessibility Shortcuts:

- Read Content of a Cell: Alt + Shift + A

- Speak Cells: Alt + Shift + S

12. Developer Shortcuts:

- Open VBA Editor: Alt + F11
- Run Macro: Alt + F8

13. Ribbon & Quick Access Toolbar Shortcuts:

- Navigate Ribbon with Keyboard: Alt (then follow key tips)
- Customize Quick Access Toolbar: Alt + F + T

14. Comment and Note Shortcuts:

- Insert Comment: Shift + F2
- Show/Hide Comments: Shift + F10 + H

15. Text Alignment Shortcuts:

- Align Text Left: Alt + H + A + L
- Align Text Center: Alt + H + A + C
- Align Text Right: Alt + H + A + R

16. Grouping and Ungrouping Shortcuts:

- Group Rows or Columns: Alt + Shift + Right Arrow
- Ungroup Rows or Columns: Alt + Shift + Left Arrow

17. Fill Shortcuts:

- Fill Down from Cell Above: Ctrl + D

- Fill Right from Cell Left: Ctrl + R

18. Special Paste Options:

- Paste Values Only: Alt + E + S + V
- Paste Formats Only: Alt + E + S + T

19. Display Shortcuts:

- Show Formulas instead of Values: Ctrl + ' (grave accent key)
- Turn on/off Gridlines: Alt + W + G

20. Miscellaneous Shortcuts:

- Create a Table: Ctrl + T
- Insert Hyperlink: Ctrl + K
- Toggle Full-Screen Mode: Alt + W + E

21. Calculation Shortcuts:

- Calculate All Open Workbooks: F9
- Calculate Active Worksheet: Shift + F9

22. Filter Shortcuts:

- Clear Filter from Current Column: Alt + Down Arrow, C

23. Special Cell Selection Shortcuts:

- Go to Special Cells Dialog Box: Ctrl + G

- Select All Cells with Comments: Alt + S, C
- Select All Cells with Formulas: Alt + S, F

24. 3D Reference Shortcuts:

- Move Between Workbooks: Ctrl + Tab
- Move Between Workbooks in Reverse Order: Ctrl + Shift + Tab

25. AutoFormat Shortcuts:

- Apply AutoFormat: Alt + H, L, P
- Choose AutoFormat: Alt + H, L, S

26. Print Preview and Page Setup Shortcuts:

- Print Preview: Ctrl + F2
- Open Page Setup Dialog Box: Alt + P, S, P

27. Spellcheck and Grammar Shortcuts:

- Check Spelling: F7
- Research Pane: Alt + Click on a word

28. Accessibility Shortcuts:

- Activate Access Keys: Alt or F10
- Move to Ribbon Commands: Tab or Shift + Tab
- Access File Tab: Alt + F

29. Collaboration Shortcuts:

- Share Workbook: Alt + F, D, S
- Track Changes: Alt + R, T, G

30. Advanced Filter Shortcuts:

- Open Advanced Filter Dialog: Alt + A, Q

31. Cell Styles and Formatting:

- Open Cell Style Menu: Alt + H, L, S

32. Conditional Formatting Shortcuts:

- Open Conditional Formatting Menu: Alt + H, L, H

33. Name Manager and Defining Names:

- Open Name Manager: Ctrl + F3
- Define Name: Ctrl + Alt + F3

34. Data Validation Shortcuts:

- Open Data Validation Dialog: Alt + D, L

35. Macro and VBA Shortcuts:

- Record Macro: Alt + L, R, R
- Relative Reference While Recording: Alt + L, R, W

36. Header and Footer Shortcuts:

- Insert Page Number in Footer: Alt + N, U, P
- Insert Number of Pages in Footer: Alt + N, U, N

Remember, practice makes perfect. The more you use these shortcuts, the more natural they will become, leading to more efficient data handling.

New Features

In addition to new functions, Excel 2023 also introduces several new features that enhance the user experience:

- **Formula Value Preview Tooltip**: This feature, available for both Windows and Mac users, provides a preview of the value a formula will return before you commit to entering it. This feature can help you verify that your formulas are correct before you finalize them.
- **Check Performance**: This feature, available for web users, allows you to speed up large workbooks. It provides insights into what might be slowing down your workbook and offers suggestions for improving performance.
- **Formula Argument Assistance**: This feature, available for web users, helps you insert and edit formulas more effectively by providing assistance with formula arguments.
- **Drag & Drop in Queries Pane**: This feature, available for web users, enhances your query organization capabilities. You can now easily rearrange queries in the Queries Pane using drag and drop.
- **Block Untrusted XLL Add-Ins**: This security feature, available for Windows users, allows you to block untrusted

XLL add-ins, enhancing the security of your Excel workbooks.

These new functions and features in Excel 2023 significantly enhance the program's capabilities, making it an even more powerful tool for data analysis and manipulation.

Additional Resources for Excel Mastery

To further enhance your Excel skills, consider the following resources:

1. Microsoft's Official Excel Training: Microsoft offers free online training for Excel that covers basic to advanced concepts.

2. ExcelJet: ExcelJet offers a wide range of tutorials, articles, and tips to help you become an Excel power user.

3. Chandoo.org: Chandoo.org provides a variety of Excel tutorials and templates to help you understand and use Excel more effectively.

4. MrExcel.com: MrExcel.com offers a forum where you can ask questions and get answers from Excel experts.

5. Excel Easy: Excel Easy offers free tutorials and downloadable examples to help you learn Excel at your own pace.
   Remember, mastering Excel is a journey. The more you use and explore the program, the more proficient you will become. Happy Excelling!

Appendix

Excel 2023 Function Reference Guide

Microsoft Excel, a widely used spreadsheet program, is continuously updated with new features and functions to enhance data analysis and manipulation. The 2023 version of Excel is no exception, offering a plethora of functions to help users manage and analyze their data more effectively. This guide provides a comprehensive overview of the functions available in Excel 2023, categorized by their primary use.

1. Text Functions

Text functions in Excel are used to manipulate or create strings of text.

- 'CONCAT': This function combines two or more text strings into one text string.
    - 'LEFT': This function returns the first character or characters in a text string, based on the number of characters you specify.

- 'RIGHT': This function returns the last character or characters in a text string, based on the number of characters you specify.

- 'MID': This function returns a specific number of characters from a text string, starting at the position you specify.

- 'LEN': This function returns the number of characters in a text string.

- 'FIND': This function returns the starting position of a specific text string within another text string.

- 'REPLACE': This function replaces part of a text string with a different text string.

- 'SUBSTITUTE': This function substitutes new text for old text in a text string.

2. Logical Functions

Logical functions in Excel are used to perform logical tests and return appropriate values.

- 'IF': This function returns one value if a condition is true and another value if it's false.

- 'AND': This function returns TRUE if all its arguments are true; returns FALSE if one or more argument is false.

- 'OR': This function returns TRUE if any argument is true; returns FALSE if all arguments are false.

- 'NOT': This function reverses the logic of its argument.

- 'IFERROR': This function returns a value you specify if a formula evaluates to an error; otherwise, it returns the result of the formula.

- 'IFS': This function checks multiple conditions and returns a value corresponding to the first TRUE condition.

3. Date and Time Functions

Date and time functions in Excel are used to create and manipulate dates and times.

- 'DATE': This function returns the sequential serial number that represents a particular date.
   - 'TIME': This function returns the decimal number for a particular time.
   - 'NOW': This function returns the current date and time.
   - 'TODAY': This function returns the current date.
   - 'DAY': This function converts a serial number to a day of the month.
   - 'MONTH': This function converts a serial number to a month.
   - 'YEAR': This function converts a serial number to a year.
   - 'HOUR': This function converts a serial number to an hour.
   - 'MINUTE': This function converts a serial number to a minute.
   - 'SECOND': This function converts a serial number to a second.

4. Lookup and Reference Functions

Lookup and reference functions in Excel are used to find specific data in a table or range by row.

- 'VLOOKUP': This function looks for a value in the leftmost column of a table, and then returns a value in the same row from a column you specify.
   - 'HLOOKUP': This function looks for a value at the top of a

table or array and returns the value in the same column from a row you specify.

- 'INDEX': This function returns a value or the reference to a value from within a table or range.

- 'MATCH': This function searches for a specified item in a range of cells, and then returns the relative position of that item in the range.

- 'OFFSET': This function returns a reference to a range that is a specified number of rows and columns from a cell or range of cells.

5. Mathematical Functions

Mathematical functions in Excel are used to perform various mathematical calculations.

- 'SUM': This function adds all the numbers in a range of cells.

- 'AVERAGE': This function returns the average (arithmetic mean) of the arguments.

- 'MIN': This function returns the smallest number in a set of values.

- 'MAX': This function returns the largest number in a set of values.

- 'COUNT': This function counts the number of cells that contain numbers, and counts numbers within the list of arguments.

- 'ROUND': This function rounds a number to a specified number of digits.

- 'SQRT': This function returns a positive square root.

- 'ABS': This function returns the absolute value of a number.

6.VStack and HStack Functions

The **VSTACK** and **HSTACK** functions are new to Excel 2023 and provide enhanced capabilities for working with arrays.

- **VSTACK**: This function combines arrays vertically into a single array. Each subsequent array is appended to the bottom of the previous array. This function is particularly useful when you need to stack data from multiple ranges vertically.
- **HSTACK**: This function combines arrays horizontally into a single array. Each subsequent array is appended to the left of the previous array. This function is beneficial when you need to stack data from multiple ranges horizontally.

7. TextSplit and TextBefore Functions

The **TEXTSPLIT** and **TEXTBEFORE** functions are new additions to Excel's text functions.

- **TEXTSPLIT**: This function splits a text string with a given delimiter into multiple values. The output from **TEXTSPLIT** is an array that will spill into multiple cells in the workbook. This function is a powerful tool for splitting text into multiple cells based on a specific delimiter.
- **TEXTBEFORE**: This function extracts text that occurs before a given delimiter. This function can be useful when you need to extract a specific portion of a text string based on a delimiter.

This guide is by no means exhaustive. Excel 2023 offers a vast array of functions, each designed to perform specific tasks. For a more comprehensive list and detailed explanations of each function, refer to the official Microsoft Excel documentation.

Made in United States
Troutdale, OR
10/06/2023

13456468R00116